Experimental Storytelling

Pushing Boundaries
and Redefining Literary Art

A Little Tree Food Forest Publication

Researched & Written with ChatGPT

Printed in the United States of America

ISBN 9798861155359

Table of Contents

Introduction
Breaking the Mold

Welcome to the world of "Experimental Storytelling: Pushing Boundaries and Redefining Literary Art." In the vast and ever-evolving landscape of literature, the power of storytelling has captivated the human imagination for centuries. From the epic poems of Homer to the timeless novels of Jane Austen and the contemporary masterpieces of Haruki Murakami, storytelling has been a vessel for transporting readers to distant realms, exploring complex emotions, and challenging our perspectives on life, love, and the human condition.

Yet, as we embark on this literary journey, we invite you to leave behind the familiar shores of conventional storytelling and venture into uncharted waters. The pages ahead will introduce you to a world where narratives are not bound by the constraints of linear time, where words transcend the limitations of the page, and where characters defy the boundaries of convention. This book is a celebration of the avant-garde, the daring, and the innovative—a testament to the power of words to transcend their traditional roles and become art in their own right.

To understand the significance of experimental storytelling, we must first look back in time and trace the evolution of storytelling itself. Storytelling is not a static art form; it is a living, breathing entity that has adapted and transformed over millennia. From the oral traditions of ancient civilizations to the invention of the printing press and the digital revolution of the 21st century, storytelling has continuously pushed the boundaries of human expression.

In Chapter 1, we'll explore the roots of storytelling, from the earliest cave paintings to the epic tales passed down through generations. We'll delve into how stories have shaped cultures, conveyed knowledge, and forged connections between people across time and space. By understanding the rich history of storytelling, we gain valuable insights into why experimentation has always been an essential aspect of the craft.

Before we can embark on our exploration of experimental storytelling, we must define our terms. What exactly do we mean when we say "experimental storytelling"? Is it a rejection of traditional storytelling, or is it an evolution of it? In Chapter 2, we'll clarify these questions and establish a working definition of experimental storytelling.

We'll examine how experimental storytelling challenges the established norms of narrative structure, character development, and language use. This chapter serves as our compass, guiding us through the uncharted territory of innovative storytelling techniques and shedding light on why these experiments are not just whimsical but vital to the evolution of literature.

Why should we, as writers and readers, care about pushing the boundaries of storytelling? What's at stake if we stick to the tried-and-true formulas? Chapter 3 addresses these critical questions by highlighting the significance of experimentation in literature.

We'll explore how pushing boundaries can lead to ground-breaking works of art, how it challenges the status quo, and how it reflects the ever-changing nature of human experience. Through examples and anecdotes, we'll illustrate how experimental storytelling has the power to evoke emotions, provoke thought, and inspire change, making it a cornerstone of literary innovation.

As we set sail on this literary voyage, remember that the pages that follow are not a rule book but an invitation—a call to adventure. We invite you to immerse yourself in the world of experimental storytelling, to question the conventions, to celebrate the unconventional, and to redefine the boundaries of literary art. Whether you're a seasoned writer looking for fresh inspiration or a curious reader eager to explore uncharted literary realms, this book is your guide to a world where storytelling knows no bounds.

So, without further ado, let us embark on a journey into the heart of experimental storytelling, where the rules are rewritten, and the possibilities are limitless. Together, we will uncover the secrets of this captivating art form, and in doing so, we may just discover new dimensions of our own creativity and imagination. Welcome to the future of literature.

Chapter 1
The Evolution of Storytelling

Before we plunge into the depths of experimental storytelling, it's essential to trace our footsteps back in time, to the very origins of storytelling. To understand where we're going, we must first comprehend where we've come from. The evolution of storytelling is a captivating journey that stretches across centuries, continents, and cultures, weaving a tapestry of human creativity, communication, and imagination.

The Primordial Fireside Tales

Picture yourself in the distant past, sitting around a flickering campfire. The stars twinkle overhead, and the night is alive with the sounds of the wilderness. Here, in this ancient setting, the earliest forms of storytelling took shape. Long before the invention of the written word, our ancestors shared their experiences, wisdom, and dreams through the spoken word.

These primordial stories weren't just entertainment; they were essential tools for survival. Tales of hunting, gathering, and navigating the treacherous landscapes of our world were passed down from generation to generation. These stories taught crucial lessons about food, shelter, and the dangers lurking in the shadows.

The Birth of Myth and Legend

As societies grew more complex, so did the stories

they told. Mythology and legend emerged as humanity's first attempts to explain the mysteries of existence. Gods and heroes became central figures, and stories became a means of exploring the human condition and the world's wonders.

In ancient Mesopotamia, the epic of Gilgamesh recorded the adventures of a legendary hero-king and his quest for immortality. Meanwhile, the Greek pantheon of gods inspired epic tales like the Iliad and the Odyssey, capturing the essence of human struggle, heroism, and hubris.

The Power of the Written Word

The development of written language marked a transformative chapter in the history of storytelling. Writing allowed stories to transcend the boundaries of oral tradition, making them immortal on the pages of parchment and papyrus. From the hieroglyphics of ancient Egypt to the cuneiform script of Mesopotamia, civilizations around the world began to record their myths, histories, and insights.

One pivotal moment in this narrative was the invention of the printing press by Johannes Gutenberg in the 15th century. This revolutionary technology democratized access to written stories, making books more widely available than ever before. The Gutenberg Bible, with its beautifully crafted print, stands as a symbol of this turning point in human communication.

Literature's Renaissance and Enlightenment

The Renaissance witnessed a flourishing of storytelling as artists and writers embraced new forms of expression. William Shakespeare's plays, such as "Romeo and Juliet" and "Hamlet," transcended language barriers and continue to captivate audiences today. The 18th-century Enlightenment further fueled the exchange of ideas through literature, promoting reason, science, and individualism.

The Birth of the Novel

The novel, as a distinct literary form, came into its own in the 18th century. Novels like Daniel Defoe's "Robinson Crusoe" and Jane Austen's "Pride and Prejudice" provided readers with in-depth character studies and intricate plots. The novel allowed for a more extended exploration of human psychology, relationships, and societal dynamics.

The 20th Century: Breaking New Ground

The 20th century marked a period of profound experimentation and innovation in storytelling. Writers like James Joyce challenged traditional narrative structures with works like "Ulysses," employing stream-of-consciousness techniques that invited readers into the minds of characters. Virginia Woolf's "Mrs. Dalloway" explored the inner thoughts of its characters in a stream of consciousness, blurring the lines between thoughts and narration.

As we delve deeper into the 20th century and beyond, we'll encounter the explosion of postmodern literature, characterized by authors like Jorge Luis Borges and Italo Calvino. These writers questioned the very nature of storytelling itself, often weaving metafictional narratives that playfully explored the boundaries between reality and fiction.

A Journey Through Time

The history of storytelling is a winding river, flowing

through epochs, cultures, and artistic movements. It is a testament to the human need to communicate, to share experiences, and to make sense of the world. Our journey through time has shown us how storytelling has evolved, from the primitive fireside tales to the experimental narratives of the modern age.

As we navigate the uncharted waters of experimental storytelling in this book, remember that we are building on this rich tapestry of tradition and innovation. We are standing on the shoulders of giants — those storytellers who dared to challenge the status quo, push boundaries, and redefine what it means to tell a story.

So, dear reader, with this historical backdrop in mind, let's embark on our exploration of experimental storytelling. Our journey has only just begun, and the most exciting chapters await us. In the pages ahead, we will discover how storytelling has continued to evolve, morphing into new and daring forms that push the boundaries of literature and ignite the imagination.

Chapter 2
What is Experimental Storytelling?

Now that we've taken a glimpse into the evolutionary history of storytelling, let's embark on a journey into the heart of our subject: experimental storytelling. What exactly is it, and why is it worth exploring? In this chapter, we'll shine a spotlight on the essence of experimental storytelling, dissecting its components and understanding its significance in the literary world.

Breaking the Mold: A Definition

At its core, experimental storytelling represents a departure from the traditional conventions of storytelling. It's a rebellion against the tried-and-true, an audacious adventure into uncharted narrative territory. But what precisely does it entail?

1. Challenging Narrative Structure

In the realm of experimental storytelling, the linear progression of a narrative isn't gospel. Stories don't necessarily start at point A, journey through events sequentially, and reach point B. Instead, experimental storytellers may employ nonlinearity, fractured timelines, and fragmented narratives. Imagine a story that begins at its climax, then jumps backward and forward in time, leaving the reader to piece together the puzzle. This disruption of linear structure can create suspense, invite deeper exploration, and challenge our perception of time itself.

2. Playing with Language and Form

Traditional storytelling often adheres to conventional language and format. In contrast, experimental storytellers use language as a playground. They may employ poetic prose, wordplay, and linguistic acrobatics to craft narratives that are as much about the texture of language as they are about plot. Visual experimentation also plays a crucial role. Think of stories that incorporate illustrations, typography, or even multimedia elements to immerse readers in a multisensory experience.

3. Shaping Characters in New Ways

In experimental storytelling, characters can transcend the typical archetypes and become complex, multi-dimensional beings. Expect to encounter unreliable narrators, antiheroes, and characters who blur the line between protagonist and antagonist. These unconventional characters invite readers to question their own judgments, beliefs, and biases, leading to a deeper engagement with the narrative.

4. Pushing the Boundaries of Genre

Genres often serve as cozy containers for stories, but experimental storytellers revel in pushing those boundaries. They may blend genres with abandon, mixing elements of science fiction, fantasy, and realism, or they might craft entirely new genres that defy classification. The result is a literary landscape where rules are rewritten and readers are kept on their toes.

The Quest for Innovation

"Why experiment?" you might ask. What's the point of challenging storytelling conventions? Well, that's where the magic happens. The act of experimentation isn't merely an exercise in novelty; it's a quest for innovation, a drive to uncover new dimensions of storytelling.

1. Provoking Thought

Experimental storytelling doesn't spoon-feed readers. It invites them to participate actively in the narrative, challenging them to interpret, question, and engage with the text on a deeper level. By disrupting familiar patterns, it prompts reflection and critical thinking, leaving a lasting impact.

2. Reflecting Complexity

The world is a complex place, and traditional narratives can sometimes oversimplify it. Experimental storytelling, with its intricate characters, nonlinearity, and unconventional forms, mirrors the intricacies of real life. It embraces ambiguity, paradox, and the messy, contradictory nature of human existence.

3. Expanding Creative Horizons

For writers, experimenting with storytelling techniques can be liberating. It's an opportunity to break free from the constraints of formulaic storytelling and explore the limitless possibilities of language and narrative. It allows authors to find their unique voices and push the boundaries of their creative potential.

A Spectrum of Experimentation

It's important to note that experimental storytelling isn't a monolithic entity. It's a spectrum, with a wide range of techniques and approaches. Some experiments are subtle, gently nudging at the edges of convention, while others are bold and radical, shattering the mold entirely.

Throughout this book, we'll explore various forms of experimentation, from nonlinearity and unconventional formats to character exploration and metafiction. We'll encounter the avant-garde, the quirky, and the thought-provoking, all in the name of pushing the boundaries of literature.

As we continue our journey through these pages, remember that experimental storytelling is an invitation — an invitation to challenge preconceived notions, to embrace the unconventional, and to embark on a literary adventure that knows no bounds. So, fasten your seat belt, dear reader; we're about to dive deep into the heart of experimental storytelling, where innovation thrives, and imagination knows no limits.

Chapter 3
The Importance of Pushing Boundaries

In the previous chapters, we've explored the history and definition of experimental storytelling. Now, let's delve into why pushing the boundaries of storytelling is not only a fascinating endeavor but also a vital one in the world of literature. Why should we care about experimentation, and what does it bring to the table?

A Catalyst for Progress

Innovation has been the driving force behind human progress throughout history. Think about it: from the wheel to the printing press to the smart phone, each innovation has fundamentally changed the way we live, communicate, and interact with the world. The same principle applies to storytelling.

Pushing the boundaries of storytelling is a catalyst for progress in literature. It challenges the status quo and forces us to rethink the way stories are told. By embracing experimentation, we open doors to new narrative possibilities, expand the limits of creativity, and create a more vibrant and dynamic literary landscape.

Exploring the Uncharted Territory of Emotion

Stories are not just tales; they are emotional journeys. They have the power to evoke a wide range of feelings—joy, sorrow, anger, empathy, and more. Experimental storytelling takes this emotional journey to the next level. It allows us to explore the uncharted territory of emotion by presenting familiar themes and experiences in fresh and unexpected ways.

Imagine a story that uses unconventional narrative techniques to convey the disorientation and confusion of a character suffering from memory loss. The reader becomes immersed in the character's emotional state, experiencing it firsthand. These unique emotional experiences can foster empathy, provoke thought, and leave a profound impact on the reader.

A Mirror to Our Complex World

The world we live in is far from simple. It's filled with nuance, contradiction, and ambiguity. Yet, traditional storytelling often simplifies this complexity for the sake of clarity and familiarity. Experimental storytelling, on the other hand, embraces the intricacies of our world.

By reflecting the complexity of human experiences and relationships, experimental storytelling becomes a mirror to our complex world. It acknowledges that life doesn't always follow a neat, linear narrative and that emotions are often messy and contradictory. Through unconventional characters, nonlinear narratives, and innovative forms, it captures the depth and richness of our human experience.

Fostering Critical Thinking

One of the most valuable aspects of experimental storytelling is its ability to foster critical thinking. It challenges readers to actively engage with the narrative, to question assumptions, and to interpret the story in their own unique ways. This engagement goes beyond the passive consumption of a traditional narrative; it requires active participation and interpretation.

When readers encounter nonlinearity, unreliable narrators, or unconventional formats, they are prompted to think critically about the text. They must piece together fragments of the story, consider multiple perspectives, and make connections. This cognitive engagement not only enhances their reading experience but also strengthens their analytical skills, making them more adept at navigating the complexities of the world around them.

A Lens for Cultural and Social Commentary

Experimental storytelling often serves as a powerful lens for cultural and social commentary. By pushing the boundaries of narrative structure and character development, it can shed light on societal issues, challenge stereotypes, and offer fresh perspectives on age-old problems.

For example, a story that employs multiple narrative perspectives can provide a more comprehensive view of a complex social issue, such as racial inequality or gender dynamics. By presenting the experiences of different characters, it encourages readers to empathize with diverse viewpoints and engage in meaningful conversations about these topics.

The Catalyst for Change

Throughout history, literature has played a pivotal role in inspiring change, challenging norms, and shaping societies. Think of books like "Uncle Tom's Cabin" by Harriet Beecher Stowe, which fueled the abolitionist movement, or "The Feminine Mystique" by Betty Friedan, which ignited the second-wave feminist movement.

Experimental storytelling has the potential to

be a catalyst for change in its own right. By pushing boundaries, it can draw attention to pressing issues, challenge the status quo, and inspire readers and writers to think differently. It's a tool for social commentary, a platform for marginalized voices, and a means of addressing the complexities of our modern world.

A Call to Creativity

Beyond its role in society and culture, experimental storytelling is a call to creativity. It invites writers to break free from the constraints of formulaic storytelling and explore the limitless possibilities of language and narrative. It encourages them to find their unique voices and to innovate.

For writers, experimenting with storytelling techniques can be a deeply rewarding experience. It's a chance to grow, to develop one's craft, and to contribute to the evolution of literature. Just as artists have explored new techniques and styles throughout history, so too can writers push the boundaries of their art form.

Navigating Uncharted Waters

In this chapter, we've explored the vital role that pushing the boundaries of storytelling plays in the world of literature. From fostering progress and emotional depth to reflecting complexity and promoting critical thinking, experimental storytelling is a force for innovation and change.

As we journey through the pages of this book, keep in mind that experimentation is not a rejection of tradition but an evolution of it. It's a celebration of creativity and a testament to the enduring power of storytelling. So, as we continue our exploration of experimental storytelling, embrace the uncharted waters ahead. We are about to dive deeper into the heart of this creative realm, where boundaries are meant to be pushed, and where imagination knows no limits.

Chapter 4
Embracing Nonlinear Time

Time, that ever-flowing river, is a fundamental element of storytelling. In most narratives, time marches forward in a linear fashion, carrying characters and events along with it. But what happens when we decide to play with time, to break free from the chronological shackles that bind our stories? Welcome to the world of nonlinear time in experimental storytelling.

Breaking the Chronological Mold

Linear storytelling, where events unfold in a clear sequence from beginning to end, is the most common narrative structure. It's familiar, easy to follow, and has been the backbone of storytelling for centuries. However, experimental storytelling dares to challenge this convention.

In nonlinear storytelling, time isn't a strict arrow pointing forward. Instead, it's a vast canvas that authors can paint on freely. This means stories can start at the end and work their way back, jump between different time periods, or exist in a fractured, non-sequential state. The result is a narrative structure that can be as complex and layered as real life itself.

The Allure of Nonlinearity

So, why embrace nonlinear time in storytelling? What does it bring to the narrative table?

1. Suspense and Mystery

Nonlinear storytelling can be a masterful tool for creating suspense and intrigue. When readers encounter a story that begins with a climactic scene or a mysterious event, they're immediately hooked. They're left wondering, "How did we get here?" This narrative approach invites readers to become active participants, piecing together the puzzle of the story as they go along.

2. Exploration of Memory

Our memories are rarely linear; they're fragmented, selective, and colored by emotions. Nonlinear storytelling mirrors this aspect of human memory. It allows authors to explore the way characters remember and interpret events, revealing how our past experiences shape our present actions and perceptions.

3. Multiple Perspectives

Nonlinear narratives can offer readers multiple perspectives on a single event. Picture a story where the same event is viewed through the eyes of different characters, each with their own interpretation and emotions. This technique deepens character development and invites readers to consider the subjective nature of truth.

4. Unveiling Complex Relationships

Complex relationships often involve a mix of past and present interactions, memories, and unresolved issues. Nonlinear storytelling can mirror the intricacies of these relationships by revealing different facets of character dynamics across various points in time. It allows authors to explore how relationships evolve, fracture, and heal over time.

5. Reflection and Revelation

By jumbling the timeline, authors can create moments of reflection and revelation. Readers may revisit an event with new information, leading to a deeper understanding of characters and their motivations. These "aha" moments can be incredibly satisfying and thought-provoking.

Examples of Nonlinear Time

Let's take a look at some famous examples of nonlinear storytelling:

1. "Memento" (2000)

Directed by Christopher Nolan, this film tells the story of a man with short-term memory loss. The narrative is presented in reverse chronological order, mirroring the protagonist's condition and immersing the audience in his disorienting world.

2. "Slaughterhouse-Five" (1969) by Kurt Vonnegut

This classic novel employs a nonlinear structure to tell the story of Billy Pilgrim, an American soldier who becomes "unstuck in time." The narrative jumps between different moments in Billy's life, highlighting the trauma of war and the fluidity of his existence.

3. "Eternal Sunshine of the Spotless Mind" (2004)

In this film, the nonlinear structure serves as a reflection of the characters' memories. As Joel undergoes a procedure to erase his memories of a failed relationship, the audience experiences his memories out of order, mimicking the fragmentation of his mind.

4. "Cloud Atlas" (2004) by David Mitchell

This novel weaves together six interconnected stories, spanning different time periods and genres. The nonlinear structure invites readers to make connections between characters and events, illustrating the idea that our actions ripple through time.

Challenges and Rewards

Embracing nonlinear time in storytelling can be exhilarating, but it's not without its challenges. Readers may need to work a bit harder to piece together the narrative puzzle, and authors must carefully manage transitions between different timelines to avoid confusion. However, the rewards are worth the effort. Nonlinear storytelling can create narratives that resonate on a profound level, challenge our perceptions of time and memory, and offer a fresh perspective on familiar themes. It invites us to see stories not as rigid structures but as dynamic, living entities with the power to transcend the limitations of linear time.

As we continue our journey through experimental storytelling, keep in mind that nonlinear time is just one tool in the toolkit of innovation. It's a reminder that storytelling is a flexible and boundless art form, capable of bending and reshaping to capture the complex, multifaceted nature of human experience. So, dear reader, embrace the nonlinearity and join us as we navigate the intricate pathways of experimental storytelling. The adventure has only just begun.

Chapter 5
Fragmented Narrative
Piecing Together the Puzzle

Imagine reading a book where the story isn't presented in a neat, linear fashion. Instead, it's fragmented, scattered, like pieces of a jigsaw puzzle waiting to be assembled. Welcome to the world of fragmented narratives—a hallmark of experimental storytelling that challenges the way we perceive and engage with stories.

A Disrupted Flow

In traditional storytelling, narratives flow smoothly from one event to the next, offering a coherent and logical progression. However, fragmented narratives disrupt this flow deliberately. They shatter the linear structure, presenting events, scenes, or perspectives out of order, forcing readers to piece together the narrative puzzle on their own.

This approach can initially be disorienting, like trying to make sense of a jigsaw puzzle with no picture on the box. But therein lies the allure—fragmented narratives engage readers in a unique way, inviting them to become active participants in constructing the story.

The Narrative Collage

Picture a narrative as a collage—a collection of fragments, each offering a glimpse into the larger picture.

Each fragment is a scene, a moment, or a perspective that contributes to the over arching narrative. These fragments may be presented in a nonlinear sequence, often with deliberate gaps, overlaps, or repetitions.

As readers, we become detectives, searching for connections and patterns, filling in the gaps with our imagination. This engagement allows us to explore the story from multiple angles, consider alternative interpretations, and experience the narrative in a way that linear storytelling cannot provide.

Creating Suspense and Tension

Fragmented narratives excel at creating suspense and tension. By withholding key pieces of information and revealing them strategically, authors can keep readers on the edge of their seats. As we piece together the puzzle, we experience a sense of discovery and anticipation, akin to solving a mystery.

The unknown becomes a powerful narrative tool. We might begin the story with an enigmatic event or image, leaving us eager to uncover its significance. With each new fragment, we inch closer to understanding the whole, and the thrill of discovery keeps us engaged.

Character Depth and Complexity

Fragmented narratives also offer a unique opportunity to explore the depth and complexity of characters. We may encounter a character at various points in their life, witnessing their evolution and transformation. This multifaceted perspective allows us to delve into their psyche, motivations, and internal conflicts.

Think of a character who appears first as a child, then as an adult, and later as an elderly person. The fragmented narrative allows us to witness the character's growth and changing perspectives, fostering a deeper connection with their journey and experiences.

Filling in the Blanks

One of the joys of fragmented narratives is the act of filling in the blanks. Readers become active participants in constructing the story's meaning. As we piece together the fragments, we form our own interpretations, connecting the dots and weaving a tapestry of understanding.

This process of co-creation between author and reader can be immensely rewarding. It encourages critical thinking, invites empathy, and prompts discussions about the story's themes, characters, and symbolism. Readers often find themselves drawn into the narrative, eager to uncover its secrets.

Examples of Fragmented Narratives

To better understand the concept of fragmented narratives, let's explore some notable examples:

1. "The Sound and the Fury" (1929) by William Faulkner

This novel tells the story of the Compson family from the perspectives of multiple characters, including a mentally challenged member. The narrative is fragmented, presenting events out of order and from varying viewpoints, inviting readers to piece together the family's tragic history.

2. "In the Skin of a Lion" (1987) by Michael Ondaatje

This novel blends history, romance, and fragments of memory as it explores the lives of immigrant workers in early 20th-century Toronto. The fragmented narrative creates a mosaic of experiences and perspectives, capturing the essence of a city and its people.

3. "Cloud Atlas" (2004) by David Mitchell

As mentioned in a previous chapter, this novel weaves together six distinct stories from different time periods and genres. The fragmented structure invites readers to make connections between characters and events across centuries, revealing the ripple effects of actions through time.

Challenges and Rewards

Fragmented narratives are not without their challenges. They require readers to invest time and effort in piecing together the story, and if not executed well, they can lead to confusion. Authors must strike a delicate balance between revealing enough to maintain engagement and withholding enough to create intrigue.

However, the rewards are worth it. Fragmented narratives offer a dynamic and immersive reading experience, encouraging readers to think critically, engage with characters on a deep level, and actively participate in the storytelling process. They remind us that stories can be as multifaceted and complex as the human experience itself.

As we continue our exploration of experimental storytelling, remember that fragmented narratives are just one of the many tools authors use to challenge conventions and push the boundaries of literature. So, embrace the fragments, piece together the puzzle, and join us in uncovering the beauty and complexity of experimental storytelling. The journey has only just begun.

Chapter 6
Multiple Perspectives
Seeing the Story from Different Angles

In the world of experimental storytelling, narratives aren't confined to a single viewpoint. Instead, they invite us to explore the story from multiple perspectives, offering a kaleidoscope of experiences, emotions, and interpretations. This narrative technique adds depth and complexity to storytelling, allowing us to see the story from different angles and fostering a richer understanding of characters and events.

A Symphony of Voices

Imagine a story as a symphony, and each character as an instrument. In traditional storytelling, a single instrument might dominate, drowning out the others. But in narratives with multiple perspectives, every character's voice is heard, contributing to the harmony of the whole.

Each character brings their unique viewpoint, motivations, and emotions to the narrative. They might interpret events differently, revealing hidden layers of meaning. This symphony of voices allows readers to engage with the story on a deeper level, as they witness the interplay of perspectives.

Complex Characters, Complex Worldviews

One of the most significant advantages of multiple

perspectives is the opportunity to delve into the complexity of characters. In traditional storytelling, characters are often seen primarily through the eyes of the protagonist. However, narratives with multiple perspectives invite us to step into the shoes of various characters, experiencing the story from their vantage points.

This approach humanizes characters by revealing their motivations, fears, and vulnerabilities. We gain insight into their internal struggles, their past experiences, and the forces that shape their decisions. Characters become more than heroes or villains; they become individuals with rich inner lives, making their actions and choices all the more compelling and relatable.

Redefining Empathy

Multiple perspectives also redefine empathy. When we see the story through different characters' eyes, we develop a deeper understanding of their actions and emotions. Even if we don't agree with a character's choices, we can empathize with their perspective, recognizing that their actions are often driven by their unique circumstances and beliefs.

This expanded empathy can have a profound impact on readers. It encourages them to suspend judgment, consider alternative viewpoints, and appreciate the complexity of human nature. It's a reminder that real-life conflicts often stem from differing perspectives, and empathy is a powerful tool for bridging those divides.

Revealing Unreliable Narrators

In traditional storytelling, the narrator is often assumed to be a reliable guide to the story's events. But what happens when we encounter an unreliable narrator — someone whose perspective is skewed by bias, mental state, or deception? Multiple perspectives can reveal these unreliable narrators, adding layers of intrigue and complexity to the narrative.

As readers, we become detectives, sifting through conflicting accounts to uncover the truth. We must question each character's reliability and motivation, making us active participants in unraveling the mystery. This engagement challenges us to think critically and consider the implications of unreliable narration.

Examples of Multiple Perspectives

Let's explore some famous examples of multiple perspectives in literature:

1. "The Sound and the Fury" (1929) by William Faulkner

This novel presents the story of the Compson family through the perspectives of multiple characters, each with their unique narrative style and mental state. By delving into each character's viewpoint, readers gain insight into the family's decline and tragedy.

2. "As I Lay Dying" (1930) by William Faulkner

Faulkner employs multiple perspectives once again in this novel, as each chapter is narrated by a different character. These fragmented perspectives offer a mosaic-like view of a family's journey to bury their deceased mother, highlighting the absurdity and tragedy of life.

3. "The Poisonwood Bible" (1998) by Barbara Kingsolver

This novel tells the story of a missionary family's experiences in the Congo through the perspectives of the mother and her four daughters. Each character's voice reflects their unique upbringing, beliefs, and struggles, providing a multifaceted view of colonialism and cultural clashes.

Challenges and Rewards

While multiple perspectives add depth and complexity to storytelling, they also present challenges. Managing multiple viewpoints requires careful planning to ensure each character's voice is distinct and contributes meaningfully to the narrative. The author must also strike a balance between offering diverse perspectives and maintaining coherence.

However, the rewards are immense. Multiple perspectives open doors to exploring the richness of human experience, promoting empathy, and revealing the multifaceted nature of truth. They encourage readers to engage critically with the text and to consider the multifarious ways in which people perceive and interpret the world.

A Tapestry of Perspectives

As we continue our journey through experimental storytelling, remember that multiple perspectives are a testament to the complexity of human nature and the richness of storytelling itself. They invite us to embrace diversity, question assumptions, and engage with characters on a profound level.

The narratives we encounter in this chapter are not solitary voices but threads in a larger tapestry—a tapestry of perspectives that paints a more complete picture of the human experience. So, as you immerse yourself in narratives with multiple viewpoints, consider the significance of seeing the story from different angles.

Chapter 7
The Art of Flashbacks and Flashforwards

In the ever-evolving landscape of storytelling, time is not a fixed point but a canvas where authors paint their narratives. As we delve deeper into the realm of experimental storytelling, we encounter two powerful brushes: flashbacks and flashforwards. These narrative techniques allow us to manipulate time, weaving past and future into the present, creating a tapestry of interconnected moments that challenge the conventional flow of a story.

Peering into the Past: The Art of Flashbacks

Flashbacks transport us backward in time, providing glimpses into a character's history, motivations, and the events that have shaped them. They're like windows into the past, allowing us to see how earlier experiences continue to reverberate in the present.

The Function of Flashbacks
1. Character Depth

Flashbacks are a tool for character development. By revealing a character's past, authors can add layers of complexity and nuance to their personalities. Readers gain insight into their motivations, fears, and traumas, deepening their connection to the character.

2. Plot Enrichment

Flashbacks can enrich the plot by providing context and explanation for current events. They unveil mysteries, answer questions, and offer a deeper understanding of the story's unfolding events.

3. Emotional Resonance

Flashbacks evoke emotions by allowing us to witness pivotal moments in a character's life. Whether it's a heart-wrenching loss or a transformative experience, these glimpses into the past can elicit empathy and empathy from readers.

The Art of Seamless Transition

A well-executed flashback seamlessly integrates into the narrative, feeling like a natural progression rather than a jarring interruption. Authors employ various techniques to achieve this:

1. Trigger Events

Flashbacks can be triggered by a current event or a character's internal thoughts and emotions. These triggers create a logical connection between the present and the past.

2. Transitions

Authors often use transitional phrases or imagery to signal a shift in time. These transitions serve as signposts, guiding readers through the temporal journey.

3. Voice and Tone

Authors may adopt a distinct voice or tone to set apart flashbacks from main narrative. This differentiation helps readers distinguish between past and present.

Examples of Flashbacks

Let's explore some examples of flashbacks in literature and film:

1. "The Great Gatsby" (1925) by F. Scott Fitzgerald

The novel employs flashbacks to reveal the mysterious past of its enigmatic protagonist, Jay Gatsby. These glimpses into Gatsby's earlier life provide insight into his obsession with wealth and his unrequited love for Daisy.

2. "Memento" (2000) directed by Christopher Nolan

In this film, the narrative is structured entirely as a series of flashbacks. The protagonist, suffering from short-term memory loss, pieces together his past through a disjointed series of scenes presented in reverse chronological order.

3. "The Kite Runner" (2003) by Khaled Hosseini

This novel uses flashbacks to explore the childhood friendship and subsequent betrayal between Amir and Hassan. The flashbacks are integral to understanding the characters' complex relationship.

Leaping into the Future
The Art of Flashforwards

While flashbacks dive into the past, flashforwards catapult us into the future. These narrative leaps offer a tantalizing glimpse of what's to come, setting the stage for anticipation and intrigue.

The Function of Flashforwards
1. Foreshadowing

Flashforwards serve as a form of foreshadowing,

hinting at events or outcomes that will occur later in the story. This creates suspense as readers eagerly await the fulfillment of these glimpses into the future.

2. Tension and Uncertainty

Flashforwards introduce tension by presenting a future event or scenario that raises questions. As readers navigate the narrative, they are driven to discover how the story will arrive at the depicted future.

3. Exploring Consequences

Flashforwards can explore the consequences of characters' actions or decisions. By showing the potential outcomes of choices, authors highlight the weight of decisions and their impact on the narrative.

The Element of Surprise

Flashforwards are powerful tools for surprising readers. By presenting a future event that deviates from their expectations, authors can subvert assumptions and challenge the reader's understanding of the story. This element of surprise keeps the narrative fresh and engaging.

Seamless Integration of Flashforwards

Like flashbacks, flashforwards must be seamlessly integrated into the narrative to avoid disrupting the flow. Authors employ similar techniques to achieve this:

1. Contextual Clues

Flashforwards are often introduced with contextual clues, such as time stamps or references to future events. These clues prepare readers for the temporal shift.

2. Transitions

Transitioning smoothly from the present to the future and back is essential. Authors may use transitional phrases, imagery, or shifts in narrative voice to facilitate these transitions.

3. Maintaining Suspense

Authors often balance the revelation of future events with the maintenance of suspense. While readers catch glimpses of the future, the details surrounding those events remain shrouded in mystery until the narrative catches up.

Examples of Flashforwards

Here are some examples of flashforwards in literature and film:

1. "The Curious Case of Benjamin Button" (1922) by F. Scott Fitzgerald

This short story, later adapted into a film, tells the tale of Benjamin Button, who ages backward. The narrative begins with a flashforward, showing Benjamin as an elderly infant, and then proceeds to explain how he reached that point.

2. "Lost" (TV Series, 2004-2010)

The show frequently employed flashforwards to provide glimpses into the futures of its characters. These flashforwards added layers of mystery and intrigue, as viewers tried to piece together the timeline of events.

3. "Slaughterhouse-Five" (1969) by Kurt Vonnegut

This novel is known for its unconventional structure, including flashforwards and nonlinearity. The protagonist, Billy Pilgrim, experiences moments from his future, creating a sense of inevitability and fatalism.

The Temporal Palette

As we explore the art of flashbacks and flashforwards, remember that time is not a static backdrop but a dynamic element that authors can manipulate to create diverse and engaging narratives. These techniques, when wielded skillfully, enhance storytelling by deepening character development, creating tension, and surprising readers.

So, as you encounter narratives that leap through time, whether into the past or the future, embrace the temporal palette that authors use to craft their stories. Each flash of insight into the temporal puzzle brings us closer to a deeper understanding of the narrative and a richer appreciation of the art of experimental storytelling. The journey continues, with more temporal adventures awaiting.

Chapter 8
The Visual Narrative
Art and Storytelling Combined

In the realm of experimental storytelling, words aren't the only tools at an author's disposal. Visual elements can also play a significant role in shaping narratives and expanding the boundaries of storytelling. This chapter explores the fascinating intersection of art and storytelling, where visual narratives come to life, offering readers a multisensory and immersive experience.

The Power of Visual Storytelling

Visual storytelling is a broad and dynamic field, encompassing a wide range of media and techniques, from graphic novels and comics to illustrated novels, interactive storytelling apps, and even multimedia presentations.

What unites them is their ability to convey narrative information, emotions, and themes through visual means.

The Marriage of Words and Images

Visual storytelling isn't a replacement for traditional storytelling but a complement to it. It's a marriage of words and images, where each element enhances the other. Words can provide context, inner thoughts, and dialogue, while images convey atmosphere, emotion, and visual cues.

This synergy allows visual narratives to explore complex themes and evoke powerful emotions. It transcends the limitations of language, making stories accessible to diverse audiences and offering new ways to engage with narrative content.

Graphic Novels and Comics: A Unique Art Form

Graphic novels and comics are perhaps the most well-known forms of visual storytelling. They merge illustrations with text to create a unique narrative experience. Here's why they're worth exploring:

1. Visual Language

Graphic novels and comics have their visual language, including panel layouts, speech bubbles, and onomatopoeic words. This visual vocabulary guides readers through the narrative, creating a rhythm and flow unique to the medium.

2. Character Expression

Visual storytelling excels at conveying character emotions. Facial expressions, body language, and visual cues can communicate nuances that words alone might struggle to capture. This depth of expression enhances character development and reader engagement.

3. World Building

Artists can immerse readers in vivid and imaginative worlds through detailed illustrations. These visual landscapes enrich the story's setting, adding layers of atmosphere and context.

4. Sequential Art

The act of turning pages in a graphic novel or comic creates a sense of anticipation and progression. Readers actively participate in the narrative by controlling the pacing of their reading, much like the turning of a film reel.

Examples of Visual Storytelling

Let's explore some celebrated examples of visual storytelling:

1. "Maus" (1980-1991) by Art Spiegelman

This graphic novel tells the story of Holocaust survivor Vladek Spiegelman and his experiences during World War II. The use of anthropomorphic animals to represent different groups adds a layer of symbolism and emotional resonance to the narrative.

2. "Watchmen" (1986-1987) by Alan Moore and Dave Gibbons

This ground-breaking graphic novel combines intricate artwork with a complex narrative that explores themes of power, morality, and heroism. Its layered storytelling and visual motifs invite readers to dig deep into its themes.

3. "Asterios Polyp" (2009) by David Mazzucchelli

This graphic novel is renowned for its innovative visual storytelling techniques, using color, symbolism, and design to reflect the protagonist's inner journey. It's a prime example of how visual elements can enhance the narrative.

Beyond the Page
Interactive and Multimedia Storytelling

Visual storytelling isn't confined to static pages. In the digital age, interactive and multimedia storytelling has emerged as a dynamic and immersive medium. These formats incorporate elements such as animation, sound, and interactivity to engage readers on multiple sensory levels.

Interactive Narratives

Interactive storytelling apps and games allow readers to make choices that influence the narrative's outcome. This participatory experience empowers readers to become co-creators of the story, shaping its direction and exploring multiple branching paths.

Transmedia Storytelling

Transmedia narratives expand a story across multiple media platforms, such as books, films, websites, and social media. This approach creates a rich and interconnected narrative universe that invites readers to explore and engage with the story in diverse ways.

Virtual Reality (VR) and Augmented Reality (AR)

These technologies immerse readers in a 360-degree visual and auditory environment, allowing them to step inside the story. VR and AR storytelling provide a level of immersion that traditional media cannot match.

The Multisensory Experience

One of the strengths of visual storytelling is its ability to create a multisensory experience. Readers not only see the narrative unfold but also engage with it on an emotional and sensory level. Sound, color, movement, and interactivity add layers of immersion and engagement that can be deeply impactful.

Visual Storytelling and Empathy

Visual narratives have a unique power to evoke

empathy. Seeing characters and situations depicted visually can make stories more relatable and emotionally resonant. Readers can connect with characters on a visceral level, experiencing their struggles, joys, and transformations more vividly.

Challenges and Rewards of Visual Storytelling

Visual storytelling presents its own set of challenges, from coordinating the collaboration between authors and artists to balancing the visual and textual elements effectively. However, the rewards are equally profound.

Incorporating visual storytelling into your creative arsenal allows you to:

Evoke Powerful Emotions

Visual elements, such as expressive character art and atmospheric illustrations, have the ability to tug at the heartstrings of readers. They can feel the joy, pain, and excitement of the narrative in a visceral way.

Expand Narrative Possibilities

Visual storytelling opens up a realm of creative possibilities. You can explore abstract concepts, dreamscapes, and surreal worlds that might be challenging to convey through words alone.

Reach Diverse Audiences

The universal language of visuals transcends linguistic barriers. Your story can connect with a global audience, offering a truly inclusive reading experience.

Enhance Engagement

Visual storytelling encourages readers to linger on the page, immersing themselves in the details of the artwork. This prolonged engagement can deepen their connection to the story.

Challenge Conventions

Pushing the boundaries of storytelling by incorporating visual elements challenges literary norms and keeps the art of storytelling vibrant and evolving.

As you venture into the captivating world of visual storytelling, you'll discover that it's not about choosing between words and images but about harnessing the synergy of both to create narratives that resonate deeply with your readers.

Chapter 9
Epistolary Fiction
Letters, Diaries and Beyond

Epistolary fiction is a captivating narrative technique that invites readers into the private thoughts and intimate correspondence of characters. In this chapter, we explore the world of epistolary storytelling, where letters, diaries, emails, and other written forms become the medium through which stories are told. Prepare to dive into the personal and often hidden worlds of characters as we uncover the art and allure of epistolary fiction.

The Art of Epistolary Fiction

Epistolary fiction relies on a series of documents, typically letters, diary entries, or other written communications, to convey the narrative. This format offers several distinct advantages:

1. Intimacy and Authenticity

Readers gain direct access to characters' innermost thoughts and emotions. This sense of intimacy fosters a deeper connection with the characters and their experiences.

2. Multiple Perspectives

Epistolary fiction often features multiple narrators, each with their unique voice and perspective. This multiplicity of viewpoints adds depth and complexity to

47

the narrative, as readers piece together the story from various angles.

3. Realism and Immersion

The use of letters, diaries, or other written forms creates a sense of realism and immersion. It mimics the way people communicate in the real world, making the story's world feel more tangible and believable.

4. Revealing Secrets

Characters may be more candid in their private writings than they would be in dialogue or third-person narration. This allows authors to reveal secrets, inner conflicts, and hidden truths that drive the plot forward.

Letters as Storytelling Tools

Letters are the most common vehicle for epistolary storytelling, and they come in various forms:

1. Personal Letters

These letters are typically exchanged between characters and serve as a window into their relationships and emotions. They can be used to convey love, conflict, reconciliation, or any other aspect of human interaction.

2. Unsent Letters

Characters may write letters that are never intended to be sent. These unsent missives can serve as a means for characters to process their emotions, explore their inner thoughts, or address issues they can't confront in person.

3. Historical Letters

In historical fiction, letters can provide insight into the customs, language, and social norms of a particular era.

They offer a glimpse into the past and make the historical context more vivid.

Diaries and Journals: Personal Reflections

Diaries and journals are another popular form of epistolary storytelling. They provide a space for characters to record their daily lives, thoughts, and observations. Readers become confidants, privy to the character's inner monologue and private moments.

Diaries and journals can serve various functions in the narrative:

1. Character Development

Characters' diary entries reveal their growth, evolution, and self-discovery over time. Readers witness their inner struggles, aspirations, and personal revelations.

2. Plot Advancement

Characters may use their diaries to document key events, discoveries, or mysteries central to the plot. These written records can drive the narrative forward.

3. Atmosphere and Setting

Diaries can immerse readers in a specific time and place, providing rich details about the setting, culture, and historical context.

Beyond Letters and Diaries: Modern Forms of Epistolary Fiction

While traditional letters and diaries are classic forms of epistolary fiction, modern technology has expanded the possibilities of this narrative technique. In contemporary epistolary fiction, we encounter:

1. Emails

Email exchanges between characters offer a contemporary twist on letter writing. They capture the immediacy of digital communication while still allowing for introspection and character development.

2. Text Messages

In the age of smart phones, text messages have become a popular medium for conveying dialogue and character interaction. The brevity and informality of texting create unique storytelling opportunities.

3. Blog Posts and Online Chats

Characters can maintain blogs, participate in online forums, or engage in virtual conversations. These forms of digital communication provide insight into characters' interests, hobbies, and online personas.

Examples of Epistolary Fiction

Let's explore some notable examples of epistolary fiction from various genres and time periods:

1. "Dracula" (1897) by Bram Stoker

This classic horror novel unfolds through a series of letters, diary entries, newspaper clippings, and ship logs. The epistolary format intensifies the sense of mystery and dread as characters piece together the truth about Count Dracula.

2. "The Color Purple" (1982) by Alice Walker

This Pulitzer Prize-winning novel is presented as a series of letters written by Celie, an African American woman in the early 20th century. The letters chronicle her journey from a life of abuse and oppression to one of self-discovery and empowerment.

3. "Where'd You Go, Bernadette" (2012) by Maria Semple

In this contemporary comedic novel, the narrative unfolds through a collection of emails, letters, police reports, and other documents. The fragmented narrative adds humor and intrigue as readers piece together the story of the eccentric Bernadette Fox.

Challenges and Rewards of Epistolary Fiction

Epistolary fiction offers a unique and engaging way to tell a story, but it also presents its own set of challenges:

1. Maintaining Variety

To keep the narrative fresh, authors must ensure that each letter, diary entry, or digital communication contributes meaningfully to the story and reveals new facets of character or plot.

2. Balancing Voices

In stories with multiple narrators, authors must skillfully balance the voices of different characters, ensuring each one has a distinct personality and perspective.

3. Managing Time

Epistolary narratives often require careful time management to maintain a cohesive timeline, especially when letters or messages are delayed in transit.

Despite these challenges, epistolary fiction rewards readers with a rich and immersive narrative experience. It invites us to become confidants and detectives, piecing together the story from the fragments of written communication. It celebrates the power of the written word to convey emotion, relationships, and the human condition.

As we conclude our exploration of epistolary fiction, remember that it's a testament to the enduring appeal of personal communication and the art of storytelling. Whether through letters, diaries, emails, or other forms of written expression, epistolary fiction invites us to step into the lives and minds of characters, forging connections and uncovering the stories hidden within their words. The journey continues, with more narrative treasures yet to be revealed.

Chapter 10
Choose Your Own Adventure
Interactive Storytelling

Imagine a story where you're not just a passive observer but an active participant, where the plot unfolds based on choices you make. This is the enchanting world of interactive storytelling, where readers become decision-makers, shaping the narrative's direction and outcomes. In this chapter, we'll embark on a journey through the captivating realm of interactive fiction, exploring its history, mechanics, and the limitless possibilities it offers for engagement and immersion.

The Essence of Interactive Storytelling

Interactive storytelling is a genre where readers play a pivotal role in shaping the narrative. It's like a literary adventure where every decision you make influences the story's progression, leading to multiple branching paths and a range of possible endings. Here's why interactive storytelling is a fascinating frontier in literature:

1. Reader Agency

Interactive stories empower readers to become co-authors. Your choices determine the character's actions, the plot's twists, and the ultimate outcome. This agency creates a unique and personalized reading experience.

2. Replayability

Interactive narratives often feature multiple endings, encouraging readers to revisit the story and explore alternative paths. Each play through unveils new facets of the narrative, making it a dynamic and ever-evolving experience.

3. Immersion

The interactivity of these stories immerses you deeply in the narrative world. You're not merely an observer; you're a participant, navigating the story's challenges and dilemmas as if they were your own.

The Origins of Interactive Fiction

Interactive storytelling has deep roots, dating back to the early days of literature. Some of the earliest examples include "Choose Your Own Adventure" books, which gained popularity in the 1970s and 1980s. These books presented readers with choices at key junctures, directing them to different pages based on their decisions.

One of the pioneers of interactive fiction is the computer game "Colossal Cave Adventure," created by Will Crowther in 1975. This text-based adventure game allowed players to explore a cave system, solve puzzles, and make choices that affected the outcome—a precursor to modern interactive storytelling in digital form.

Mechanics of Interactive Storytelling

At the heart of interactive storytelling are decision points, where readers must make choices that determine the story's direction. These choices can be as simple as deciding which path to take in a forest or as complex as making moral decisions with far-reaching consequences.

Here's how interactive storytelling mechanics typically work:

1. Decision Points

Throughout the narrative, you encounter decision points where you must choose between options presented in the text. Your choice leads to a specific branch of the story.

2. Consequences

Each choice you make has consequences. These consequences can be immediate, altering the current scene, or long-term, shaping the overall plot and character development.

3. Branching Paths

As you progress, the story branches into multiple paths, each with its own set of choices and outcomes. This branching structure creates a nonlinear narrative, with numerous possible routes through the story.

4. Endings

Interactive narratives often feature multiple endings, reflecting the diverse outcomes that result from your choices. Some endings may be triumphant, while others may be tragic or ambiguous.

Genres and Themes in Interactive Storytelling

Interactive storytelling spans a wide range of genres and themes, catering to diverse tastes and preferences. Some common genres include:

1. Fantasy

Explore magical realms, embark on quests, and

make decisions that impact the fate of mythical worlds.

2. Mystery
Solve crimes, uncover secrets, and navigate intricate plots as a detective or amateur sleuth.

3. Science Fiction
Embark on futuristic adventures, make ethical choices in a high-tech society, and grapple with moral dilemmas posed by advanced technology.

4. Romance
Navigate the complexities of love, relationships, and personal growth, with choices that shape your character's romantic journey.

5. Horror
Confront supernatural horrors, unravel chilling mysteries, and make life-or-death decisions in spine-tingling narratives.

Themes in interactive storytelling can be as varied as in traditional literature, including exploration of identity, morality, friendship, power, and more. The genre's flexibility allows for the exploration of themes in unique and engaging ways.

Interactive Storytelling in the Digital Age
The advent of digital technology has ushered in a new era of interactive storytelling. Video games, interactive fiction apps, and online platforms provide immersive experiences that go beyond the limitations of print.

1. Video Games

Interactive storytelling is a hallmark of video games, where players make choices that influence the game's outcome. Games like "The Witcher" series and "Life is Strange" offer rich narrative experiences with branching paths and moral dilemmas.

2. Interactive Fiction Apps

Mobile apps have given rise to a resurgence of interactive fiction. Apps like "Episode" and "Choices: Stories You Play" allow users to choose their path in visual novels and interactive stories.

3. Online Platforms

Websites like "Twine" and "Choice of Games" provide platforms for authors to create and share their interactive stories with a global audience. These platforms offer a wide range of genres and styles.

The Impact of Interactive Storytelling

Interactive storytelling has a profound impact on readers and players alike:

1. Engagement

Interactivity keeps readers engaged and invested in the narrative, encouraging them to explore different paths and endings.

2. Empathy

Making choices from a character's perspective fosters empathy and allows readers to understand different viewpoints and moral dilemmas.

3. Creativity

Interactive fiction encourages creativity, as authors must craft intricate narratives with multiple branching paths and outcomes.

4. Critical Thinking

Decision-making in interactive storytelling often requires critical thinking, problem-solving, and ethical reflection.

5. Personalization

Interactive narratives provide a highly personalized reading experience, as each reader's choices lead to a unique story.

Challenges and Rewards of Interactive Storytelling

While interactive storytelling offers unparalleled engagement, it also presents unique challenges for authors and designers:

1. Complexity

Crafting an interactive narrative with multiple branches and meaningful choices can be a complex and time-consuming endeavor.

2. Coherence

Authors must ensure that the narrative remains coherent and engaging across various branching paths, which can be a daunting task.

3. Balancing Agency

Striking the right balance between reader agency and a compelling over arching narrative is crucial for a satisfying storytelling experience.

4. Coding and Design

In digital interactive fiction, coding and design skills are often required to create seamless and user-friendly experiences.

Despite these challenges, interactive storytelling has emerged as a vibrant and evolving form of literature, bridging the gap between traditional storytelling and gaming. It invites us to explore narratives in a new light, with the power to influence outcomes and shape characters' destinies.

As we conclude our exploration of interactive storytelling, remember that the choices you make within these narratives are a reflection of your own values, curiosity, and imagination. Each choice carries consequences, and each path offers a unique perspective on the story's themes and characters. So, venture forth into the world of interactive fiction, where your adventure awaits, and where the story is yours to shape and explore. The journey continues, with endless possibilities on the horizon.

Chapter 11
Poetry as Prose
Playing with Language

When we think of poetry, we often conjure images of structured verses, rhythmic patterns, and carefully chosen words. However, poetry isn't confined solely to its traditional forms. In this chapter, we'll explore the enchanting world of prose poetry and how it allows writers to blend the best of both worlds: the vivid language and imagery of poetry with the narrative depth and storytelling of prose. Welcome to the realm where language takes on new dimensions, where every sentence is a brushstroke on the canvas of imagination.

Defining Prose Poetry

Prose poetry is a hybrid genre that defies traditional distinctions between poetry and prose. Unlike conventional poetry, which often adheres to metrical and rhyme schemes, prose poetry relies on the fluidity of prose while embracing the heightened language, symbolism, and emotional resonance typically associated with poetry.

The Beauty of the Prose Poem

Prose poetry offers a unique set of advantages and possibilities for writers:

1. Fluidity

Prose poetry lacks the structural constraints of traditional verse, allowing for a more flexible and natural flow of language. It's an ideal medium for capturing the rhythm of everyday speech.

2. Imagery

Like poetry, prose poetry excels at creating vivid imagery and sensory experiences. Writers can employ metaphors, similes, and evocative language to paint rich pictures in the reader's mind.

3. Emotion

Prose poetry delves deep into the realm of emotions, often exploring themes of love, loss, longing, and introspection. It uses the intensity of poetic language to evoke powerful feelings in readers.

4. Narrative

While prose poetry doesn't adhere to traditional storytelling structures, it can still carry narratives, characters, and themes. It's a versatile medium for crafting short stories, vignettes, and character studies.

The Origin and Evolution of Prose Poetry

The origins of prose poetry can be traced back to ancient traditions. Early forms of prose poetry appeared in works such as the essays of Michel de Montaigne and the aphorisms of Friedrich Nietzsche. These writings blended narrative and poetic elements to create a unique literary experience.

In the 19th century, poets like Charles Baudelaire and Edgar Allan Poe embraced prose poetry as a means of exploring unconventional themes and emotions.

Baudelaire's collection "Paris Spleen" is a celebrated example of this genre, capturing the essence of urban life in a poetic and narrative form.

The Contemporary Landscape of Prose Poetry

Prose poetry has evolved and thrived in the modern era, with writers experimenting with various styles and themes. Today, contemporary prose poets continue to push the boundaries of the genre, exploring diverse subjects and forms.

Some notable contemporary prose poets include:

1. Bashō

A master of haiku, Bashō also experimented with prose poetry in his travelogue "The Narrow Road to the Deep North," blending poetic observations with vivid descriptions of his journeys through Japan.

2. Amy Lowell

An American poet known for her imagist poetry, Lowell also wrote prose poetry that explored themes of love, desire, and the mysteries of existence.

3. Anne Carson

A poet and essayist, Carson's work often blurs the line between prose and poetry, creating unique and thought-provoking narratives.

Crafting Prose Poetry: Techniques and Tips

If you're intrigued by the idea of prose poetry, here are some techniques and tips to help you get started:

1. Imagery and Sensory Language

Use descriptive and evocative language to create

vivid images and engage the senses of your readers. Think about how each word contributes to the sensory experience of your prose poem.

2. Metaphor and Simile

Incorporate metaphors and similes to draw unexpected connections and add layers of meaning to your prose poem. These figurative devices can elevate your language and create resonance.

3. Rhythm and Sound

Even though prose poetry lacks traditional meter, pay attention to the rhythm and musicality of your language. Experiment with sentence length, pacing, and repetition to create a unique cadence.

4. Narrative Threads

While prose poetry doesn't require a linear plot, you can still include narrative elements or thematic threads that provide coherence and structure to your piece.

5. Exploration of Themes

Dive deep into themes that resonate with you, whether they're personal, philosophical, or societal. Prose poetry is an excellent medium for introspection and contemplation.

Examples of Prose Poetry

To better understand the diversity of prose poetry, let's explore some examples:

1. "The Snows of Kilimanjaro" by Ernest Hemingway

In this classic short story, Hemingway's prose is poetic in its beauty. It explores themes of regret, memory, and the impermanence of life.

2. "The Book of Disquiet" by Fernando Pessoa

Pessoa's work blurs the line between poetry and prose, with his "heteronyms" writing in various styles. "The Book of Disquiet" is a profound exploration of identity, solitude, and the human condition.

3. "Bluets" by Maggie Nelson

This contemporary work blends memoir, essay, and prose poetry to delve into the author's fascination with the color blue. It's a meditative and lyrical exploration of love, loss, and obsession.

Prose Poetry in Everyday Life

Prose poetry isn't confined to the realm of literature; it can also be found in everyday language and communication. Think of the heartfelt letter you write to a loved one, the eloquent description of a cherished memory, or the poetic musings in a personal journal. These moments of prose poetry enrich our lives by infusing everyday language with beauty and meaning.

A Tapestry of Words

Prose poetry invites us to view language as a versatile and expressive tool—one that can paint vivid pictures, evoke deep emotions, and weave narratives that resonate with the human experience. It defies rigid boundaries and celebrates the fluidity of expression.

As you explore the world of prose poetry, remember that each sentence is an opportunity to craft a miniature work of art, where every word carries weight and every image lingers in the reader's mind. Whether you're drawn to introspective musings, vibrant descriptions, or poignant narratives, prose poetry offers a canvas for your creativity. So, embark on your own poetic journey, and let your words flow freely, creating a tapestry of language that reflects the richness of life and the boundless possibilities of prose poetry.

Chapter 12
Antiheroes and Unreliable Narrators

In the world of literature, heroes don't always wear capes, and narrators don't always speak the truth. Welcome to the intriguing realm of antiheroes and unreliable narrators, where the lines between right and wrong blur, and the very essence of truth becomes a matter of perspective. In this chapter, we'll delve into the complexities of these narrative devices, exploring how they challenge conventional storytelling norms, invite readers to question their own judgments, and breathe life into some of the most memorable characters in literary history.

Antiheroes: The Shadows of Virtue

Traditionally, heroes have been depicted as paragons of virtue, guided by a strong moral compass and unwavering principles. However, the emergence of antiheroes in literature shattered this age-old archetype, giving rise to characters who are morally complex, flawed, and often at odds with societal norms. Let's uncover the fascinating world of antiheroes:

Defining the Antihero

An antihero is a central character who lacks the traditional heroic qualities of courage, nobility, and altruism. Instead, antiheroes possess a mix of vices, weaknesses, and questionable ethics. They may engage in morally ambiguous actions, defy societal norms, or even commit acts that would be considered reprehensible in a conventional hero.

The Appeal of Antiheroes

Antiheroes hold a unique allure for readers and viewers alike:

1. Complexity

The moral ambiguity of antiheroes adds depth to their characters. Their inner conflicts and struggles make them relatable and human, evoking empathy from audiences.

2. Realism

Antiheroes reflect the complexity of the real world, where right and wrong aren't always black and white. Their actions and decisions are often shaped by the challenging circumstances they face.

3. Subversion

Antiheroes subvert the expectations of traditional heroism, challenging societal norms and defying conventional storytelling conventions. This subversion can lead to thought-provoking narratives.

4. Character Development

Over the course of a story, antiheroes may undergo profound character development. Their journeys can be transformative, leading to growth, self-discovery, or redemption.

Examples of Antiheroes

Antiheroes have graced the pages of literature and the screens of cinema and television for generations. Here are a few iconic examples:

1. Holden Caulfield in "The Catcher in the Rye" by J.D. Salinger

Holden is a disenchanted and disillusioned teenager who defies societal norms. He's neither a traditional hero nor a villain but a complex character navigating the challenges of adolescence.

2. Walter White in "Breaking Bad" (TV Series)

Walter White is a high school chemistry teacher turned methamphetamine manufacturer. His transformation from a mild-mannered family man to a ruthless drug kingpin is a compelling exploration of the antihero archetype.

3. Macbeth in "Macbeth" by William Shakespeare

Macbeth is a tragic antihero consumed by ambition. His descent into madness and violence serves as a cautionary tale about the corrupting influence of power.

Unreliable Narrators: Shifting Sands of Truth

Narrators are the storytellers, the guides through the fictional worlds we explore. But what happens when those narrators can't be trusted? Enter the world of unreliable narrators, where the truth is elusive, and the narrative landscape is shrouded in mystery.

Defining the Unreliable Narrator

An unreliable narrator is a character who tells the story but cannot be relied upon to provide an objective or truthful account of events. This unreliability can stem from a variety of factors, including:

1. Mental Instability

Narrators with psychological issues, such as delusions, paranoia, or memory gaps, may present a skewed version of reality.

2. Deception

Some narrators intentionally deceive the reader, either to manipulate the narrative or to hide their true intentions.

3. Limited Perspective

Narrators with limited knowledge or a biased perspective may inadvertently present a one-sided or incomplete view of events.

The Intrigue of Unreliable Narration

Unreliable narrators add layers of intrigue and complexity to storytelling:

1. Reader Engagement

Readers become active participants in uncovering the truth, piecing together clues, and questioning the narrator's reliability.

2. Narrative Depth

Unreliable narration can lead to deeper explorations of themes such as perception, memory, and the fallibility of human judgment.

3. Moral Ambiguity

Unreliable narrators challenge readers to consider

the ethical implications of their actions, blurring the line between right and wrong.

4. Twists and Surprises

Unreliable narrators can deliver unexpected plot twists and surprises, keeping readers engaged and intrigued.

Examples of Unreliable Narrators

Unreliable narrators have left an indelible mark on literature. Here are a few notable examples:

1. Humbert Humbert in "Lolita" by Vladimir Nabokov

Humbert Humbert, the protagonist and narrator, is a morally reprehensible character who justifies his predatory actions through his narrative. His unreliability forces readers to grapple with the disturbing nature of his perspective.

2. Scout Finch in "To Kill a Mockingbird" by Harper Lee

Scout Finch recounts the events of her childhood in Maycomb, Alabama. While her narration is sincere and earnest, it reflects her limited understanding of the complexities of racism and injustice in her society.

3. Patrick Bateman in "American Psycho" by Bret Easton Ellis

Patrick Bateman narrates his life as a wealthy, shallow, and murderous Wall Street executive. His unreliable narration raises questions about the extent of his violence and psychosis.

Antiheroes and Unreliable Narrators in Tandem

What happens when antiheroes and unreliable narrators come together in a narrative? You get a potent combination that challenges readers to navigate the moral and narrative complexities of a story.

Exploring the Gray Areas

When an antihero serves as an unreliable narrator, the lines between right and wrong become blurred to an even greater extent. Readers must grapple not only with the character's moral ambiguity but also with the uncertainty surrounding their narrative.

Creating Sympathy and Dissonance

Antiheroes as unreliable narrators can elicit complex emotional responses. Readers may simultaneously sympathize with the character's struggles and root for their redemption while also questioning their motives and actions. This emotional dissonance can lead to thought-provoking discussions about morality, empathy, and the human capacity for change.

Case Study
Rorschach in "Watchmen" by Alan Moore

A compelling example of an antihero serving as an unreliable narrator can be found in Alan Moore's graphic novel "Watchmen." Rorschach, a vigilante with a strict moral code and a fractured psyche, narrates parts of the story.

Rorschach's unreliability as a narrator stems from his extreme worldview, rigid sense of justice, and a traumatic past that has left him emotionally scarred. His moral code is unyielding, often leading him to violent and brutal actions. As he recounts events, readers are forced to confront the dissonance between his perception of justice and the ethical norms of society.

The narrative complexity deepens when readers discover Rorschach's journal, which contains his firsthand account of the story's events. This journal serves as a key plot device, raising questions about the veracity of Rorschach's claims and the extent of his unreliability.

Challenges and Rewards for Readers

Engaging with narratives featuring antiheroes and unreliable narrators can be both challenging and rewarding. These narratives encourage readers to:

1. Question Assumptions

Antiheroes and unreliable narrators compel readers to question their preconceived notions of heroism, morality, and truth.

2. Explore Morality

The moral dilemmas presented by antiheroes and unreliable narrators encourage readers to examine their own ethical principles and judgments.

3. Navigate Ambiguity

These narratives challenge readers to embrace ambiguity and appreciate the complexity of human nature and storytelling.

4. Participate Actively

Readers become active participants in the narrative, piecing together clues, interpreting actions, and making judgments.

The Power of Ambiguity

The world of antiheroes and unreliable narrators reminds us that literature is not just a reflection of a neatly ordered reality but a mirror held up to the complexities of the human experience. These narrative devices challenge us to explore the gray areas, to grapple with moral ambiguity, and to recognize that the truth, like the characters who tell it, is often multifaceted and enigmatic.

As you encounter antiheroes and unreliable narrators in your reading journey, embrace the opportunity to delve into the depths of their characters and narratives. These stories offer a rich tapestry of moral dilemmas, psychological insights, and narrative surprises. They invite you to question, reflect, and engage with storytelling in a way that transcends the boundaries of traditional heroism and objective truth. In the end, it is the ambiguity and complexity of these narratives that make them a compelling and enduring part of the literary landscape.

Chapter 13
Personification and Non-Human Protagonists

In the vast realm of storytelling, protagonists have traditionally been human beings, navigating the complexities of the human experience. But what if the central characters were not bound by flesh and blood, emotions, or the constraints of human existence? Enter the captivating world of personification and non-human protagonists, where the essence of humanity is explored through the eyes of creatures, objects, and forces of nature. In this chapter, we'll embark on a journey that challenges our understanding of identity, empathy, and the boundaries of storytelling.

Personification
Breathing Life into the Inanimate

Personification is a literary device that bestows human characteristics, emotions, and behaviors upon non-human entities, be they animals, objects, or abstract concepts. By infusing these non-human elements with human qualities, authors open the door to a unique form of storytelling that illuminates the human experience from unexpected angles.

The Power of Personification

Personification offers a multitude of creative

possibilities:

1. Empathy
Readers can relate to and empathize with non-human characters, forging connections that transcend the boundaries of species or form.

2. Metaphor and Symbolism
Personified entities often serve as powerful metaphors and symbols, shedding light on universal themes and emotions.

3. Perspective Shift
Personification allows authors to explore the world from diverse perspectives, offering fresh insights into familiar settings or themes.

4. Allegory and Satire
Personified characters and elements can be employed to convey allegorical or satirical messages, adding depth to the narrative.

Examples of Personification
The history of literature is replete with remarkable examples of personification. Here are a few notable ones:

1. The Wind in "Winnie-the-Pooh" by A.A. Milne
A blustery and opinionated character, the Wind brings personality and humor to the Hundred Acre Wood. It personifies the capricious nature of the weather.

2. Death in "The Book Thief" by Markus Zusak
Death serves as the narrator in this novel, offering a unique perspective on World War II and the human

experience. Death's narration is compassionate and contemplative.

3. The Ship in "Moby-Dick" by Herman Melville
The Pequod, Captain Ahab's ship, takes on a life of its own in Melville's classic novel. It becomes a symbol of obsession and fate, embodying both the crew's hopes and their inevitable doom.

Non-Human Protagonists
Beyond Human Experience
While personification breathes life into non-human entities, stories with non-human protagonists take us one step further. These narratives immerse us in worlds where the central characters are not human, challenging our understanding of identity, consciousness, and the essence of storytelling.

Exploring Non-Human Protagonists
Non-human protagonists open up a world of storytelling possibilities:

1. Otherness
Non-human protagonists invite readers to explore the "otherness" of their experiences, shedding light on aspects of existence that are distinct from the human perspective.

2. Empathy and Understanding
These stories encourage readers to empathize with characters who are profoundly different from themselves, fostering a sense of connection and understanding.

3. Metaphor and Allegory

Non-human protagonists can be powerful metaphors or allegorical representations, addressing complex themes and issues.

Examples of Non-Human Protagonists

Non-human protagonists have made a significant impact on literature. Here are a few remarkable examples:

1. Artificial Intelligence in "Do Androids Dream of Electric Sheep?" by Philip K. Dick

Rick Deckard, a bounty hunter tasked with "retiring" rogue androids, serves as the human protagonist. However, the story's central question revolves around the nature of humanity and consciousness, with the androids themselves as prominent characters.

2. Animals in "Watership Down" by Richard Adams

This epic adventure follows a group of rabbits as they search for a new home. The rabbits, particularly Hazel and Fiver, are fully developed characters with their own personalities and motivations.

3. The Natural World in "The Call of the Wild" by Jack London

Buck, a domesticated dog, undergoes a transformation as he adapts to the wilds of the Yukon during the Gold Rush. The story explores primal instincts and the struggle for survival.

Challenges and Rewards for Readers

Engaging with stories featuring non-human protagonists requires readers to:

1. Expand Empathy

Readers must extend their capacity for empathy beyond the human experience, connecting with characters that may be vastly different from themselves.

2. Question Assumptions

These narratives challenge preconceived notions of identity, consciousness, and the definition of "self."

3. Explore Themes Symbolically

Non-human protagonists often serve as symbolic representations, prompting readers to consider broader philosophical and societal themes.

The Vast Tapestry of Stories

Personification and non-human protagonists offer us a gateway into a world of storytelling that transcends the boundaries of human experience. These narratives encourage us to look beyond the familiar and to embrace the richness of diverse perspectives. Whether it's a talking animal, an anthropomorphic object, or an artificial intelligence, each character brings a unique lens through which we can explore the human condition, our relationship with the world, and the endless possibilities of storytelling.

As you continue your literary journey, keep an open mind to stories that challenge your understanding of what it means to be human. Personification and non-human protagonists remind us that the tapestry of stories is vast and diverse, weaving together threads of identity, empathy, and imagination. In the end, it is this diversity that makes the world of literature endlessly captivating and thought-provoking.

Chapter 14
Character Exploration
Beyond the Archetype

In the intricate tapestry of storytelling, characters are the threads that weave the narrative together. They breathe life into the pages, their complexities and nuances adding depth to the worlds they inhabit. While archetypal characters have long been a staple of literature, the art of character exploration goes beyond these stereotypes, inviting readers to connect with characters on a profound and human level. In this chapter, we'll embark on a journey that delves deep into the hearts and minds of characters, exploring how authors create individuals who defy easy categorization and resonate with readers long after the story ends.

The Archetypal Characters
Familiar Faces in Fiction

Archetypes are universal character templates that have appeared in stories across cultures and centuries. They serve as a shorthand for readers, offering instantly recognizable traits and roles. While archetypal characters have their place in literature, character exploration seeks to transcend these conventions and create individuals who are as unique as real people.

The Hero, the Villain, and the Mentor

Let's briefly explore some common archetypes:

1. The Hero

The heroic archetype is characterized by qualities such as courage, nobility, and the pursuit of justice. Heroes often embark on journeys, face challenges, and ultimately triumph over adversity.

2. The Villain

Villains are typically portrayed as antagonists who oppose the hero. They may embody qualities like greed, cruelty, and a desire for power. Their actions create conflict and tension in the story.

3. The Mentor

Mentors are wise and experienced characters who guide and support the hero on their journey. They provide guidance, teach valuable lessons, and often have a profound impact on the hero's development.

Character Exploration
The Art of Depth and Complexity

Character exploration is the process of crafting individuals who transcend archetypes and reveal the intricacies of human nature. These characters possess depth, flaws, and internal conflicts that mirror the complexity of real people.

Character Development

Character exploration involves allowing characters to grow and change throughout the story. This growth can be subtle or dramatic, but it should reflect the character's experiences, choices, and inner struggles.

Flaws and Imperfections

Perfect characters can be dull and unrelatable. Character exploration embraces flaws, insecurities, and vulnerabilities, making characters more relatable and engaging. These imperfections often drive the narrative and contribute to a character's growth.

Ambiguity and Moral Grayness

In the real world, people rarely fit neatly into categories of "good" or "evil." Character exploration acknowledges this ambiguity, allowing characters to make morally complex choices that challenge readers' expectations and beliefs.

Internal Conflicts

Characters in exploration-based narratives grapple with inner conflicts, such as doubt, fear, or conflicting desires. These struggles add depth and authenticity to their journeys.

Examples of Characters
Explored Beyond Archetypes

Let's examine a few characters who exemplify the art of character exploration:

1. Holden Caulfield in "The Catcher in the Rye" by J.D. Salinger

Holden is a complex character who defies easy classification. He struggles with alienation, grief, and a deep sense of disillusionment. His narrative voice is both poignant and humorous, allowing readers to empathize with his internal turmoil.

2. Hannibal Lecter in "The Silence of the Lambs" by Thomas Harris

Hannibal Lecter is a chilling character known for his intelligence, sophistication, and cannibalistic tendencies. While he is undoubtedly a villain, his complexity and charisma have made him a memorable and strangely compelling character.

3. Lisbeth Salander in "The Girl with the Dragon Tattoo" by Stieg Larsson

Lisbeth Salander is a brilliant hacker with a traumatic past. She is a fiercely independent and morally ambiguous character who navigates a world of crime and corruption. Her resilience and resourcefulness make her a captivating protagonist.

Challenges and Rewards for Readers

Engaging with characters explored beyond archetypes offers readers the opportunity to:

1. Connect on a Human Level

These characters resonate because they reflect the multifaceted nature of humanity, allowing readers to see themselves in their struggles and triumphs.

2. Question Assumptions

The complexity of these characters challenges preconceived notions about right and wrong, encouraging readers to consider the gray areas of morality and behavior.

3. Experience Growth

Character exploration often involves profound character development, allowing readers to witness the evolution of individuals over the course of a story.

4. Embrace Ambiguity

Ambiguous and morally complex characters invite readers to explore the intricacies of human behavior and the choices people make in challenging circumstances.

Characters as Mirrors of Humanity

Character exploration is a testament to the power of storytelling to illuminate the human condition. Through these characters, we gain insight into our own strengths, weaknesses, and moral dilemmas. They serve as mirrors, reflecting the complexity and diversity of human nature. As you continue your literary journey, seek out stories that push the boundaries of character development, inviting you to venture beyond archetypes and into the rich terrain of human experience. In these narratives, you'll discover characters who challenge, inspire, and resonate with you in ways that transcend the boundaries of fiction, reminding us that the most compelling characters are often those who feel the most real.

Chapter 15
The Metafictional Universe

Welcome to the labyrinthine world of metafiction, where the boundaries between reality and fiction blur, and storytelling becomes a hall of mirrors. In this chapter, we'll journey into the realm of metafictional narratives, where authors playfully deconstruct and manipulate the very foundations of storytelling. It's a literary adventure that challenges our understanding of fiction, blurs the lines between author and character, and invites readers to become active participants in the narrative.

Defining Metafiction: Stories About Stories

At its core, metafiction is fiction about fiction, a narrative that self-consciously acknowledges its own artificiality and invites readers to question the nature of storytelling itself. These narratives often employ a variety of techniques to achieve their metafictional goals.

Breaking the Fourth Wall

One of the most common techniques in metafiction is the breaking of the fourth wall, where characters or the narrator directly address the reader, acknowledging their existence as participants in the story. This technique can serve to draw readers into the narrative and create a sense of shared experience.

Authors as Characters

In metafiction, authors sometimes insert themselves as characters within their own stories. This blurs the line between reality and fiction, as the author becomes a participant in the world they've created.

Recursive Narratives

Metafiction often features narratives within narratives. Stories can spiral inward, with characters telling stories to other characters, creating layers of storytelling that challenge the reader to navigate a complex narrative web.

Deconstructing Genre and Tropes

Metafictional works frequently deconstruct and subvert genre conventions and literary tropes. They may playfully expose the clichés and expectations of a particular genre, inviting readers to consider how those conventions shape their reading experience.

Examples of Metafictional Works

Let's explore a few iconic examples of metafiction in literature:

1. "If on a winter's night a traveler" by Italo Calvino

This novel is a complex metafictional narrative that follows the reader's journey to find a complete book. It alternates between the main narrative, where the reader interacts with various characters, and chapters that are meant to be the beginnings of different novels. Calvino engages readers directly, making them an integral part of the story.

2. "Pale Fire" by Vladimir Nabokov

"Pale Fire" is a novel presented as a 999-line poem written by a fictional poet, John Shade, along with commentary and annotations by a character named Charles Kinbote. As readers delve into the narrative, they discover layers of deception, interpretation, and unreliable narration.

3. "House of Leaves" by Mark Z. Danielewski

This novel is a labyrinthine exploration of a family's encounter with a mysterious house that is larger on the inside than it is on the outside. The narrative is presented as a scholarly analysis of a documentary film, with footnotes, multiple narrators, and typographical experiments that challenge the reader's perception of reality.

Challenges and Rewards for Readers

Engaging with metafictional narratives offers readers unique challenges and rewards:

1. Intellectual Puzzle

Metafictional works often present intellectual puzzles and mysteries for readers to unravel, inviting them to actively engage with the text.

2. Reflection on Storytelling

Metafiction encourages readers to reflect on the nature of storytelling, the role of the author, and the act of reading itself.

3. Exploration of Identity

Characters who question their existence or authors who insert themselves into their narratives raise questions about identity and the relationship between creator and creation.

4. Experiencing Multiple Realities

Readers of metafiction may find themselves navigating multiple layers of reality within a single narrative, which can be both disorienting and intellectually stimulating.

The Endless Play of Narratives

Metafiction takes storytelling to new dimensions, pushing the boundaries of what fiction can achieve. It challenges our assumptions about narrative structure, the author's authority, and the boundaries between fiction and reality. By engaging with metafictional works, readers embark on a literary journey that is as much about self-discovery and exploration as it is about the narratives themselves.

As you delve into the world of metafiction, embrace the sense of wonder and intellectual curiosity it inspires. These narratives remind us that stories are not confined to the page but are dynamic, ever-evolving constructs that reflect the boundless creativity of human imagination. In the end, the metafictional universe invites us to become not just readers but active participants in the ongoing play of narratives that shape our understanding of the world and ourselves.

Chapter 16
Story Within a Story
Nested Narratives

Imagine a set of Russian nesting dolls, each containing a smaller doll within it. Now, apply this concept to storytelling, where narratives are layered, each containing another story within it. Welcome to the enchanting world of nested narratives, where tales multiply like echoes in a hall of mirrors. In this chapter, we'll explore the art of nested narratives, where authors weave stories within stories, inviting readers to navigate a labyrinth of narratives and uncover hidden truths.

Defining Nested Narratives: Stories in Layers

Nested narratives, also known as frame narratives or stories within stories, are a literary technique where a primary narrative contains one or more embedded narratives. These embedded narratives can take various forms, such as stories told by characters within the main story, diaries, letters, or even dreams and hallucinations.

The Structure of Nested Narratives

A nested narrative typically consists of the following elements:

1. Primary Narrative

This is the outermost layer of the story, where

the main plot and central characters are introduced. The primary narrative provides the framework for the embedded narratives.

2. Embedded Narrative

Within the primary narrative, one or more embedded narratives are presented. These can be stories told by characters, recounted events, or even documents discovered within the main narrative.

3. Narrator(s)

Each narrative layer may have its own narrator or storyteller, providing a distinct perspective and voice. The narrator of the primary narrative may also comment on or interpret the embedded narratives.

The Art of Unfolding

Nested narratives are like a set of intricately nested boxes, waiting to be opened. They create a sense of anticipation as readers peel back the layers, one story leading to another. This unfolding of narratives adds depth and complexity to the reading experience.

Examples of Nested Narratives

Let's explore some classic examples of nested narratives in literature:

1. "One Thousand and One Nights" (Arabian Nights)

This collection of Middle Eastern folktales is perhaps one of the most famous examples of nested narratives. The frame story features Scheherazade, who tells her husband, King Shahryar, stories each night to delay her execution. Within Scheherazade's tales, characters often tell their own stories, creating layers of storytelling.

2. "Frankenstein" by Mary Shelley

In this novel, the primary narrative is presented as a series of letters written by Robert Walton, an Arctic explorer, to his sister. Within Walton's letters, Victor Frankenstein recounts his life story and the creation of the creature. Victor's narrative is, in essence, an embedded narrative within the frame story.

3. "Heart of Darkness" by Joseph Conrad

In this novella, the primary narrative features Marlow, who recounts his journey up the Congo River. Within Marlow's narrative, he hears and shares the story of Kurtz, a man who has gone deep into the heart of the African wilderness and into madness. Kurtz's story is embedded within Marlow's narrative.

Challenges and Rewards for Readers

Engaging with nested narratives offers readers unique challenges and rewards:

1. Navigating Complexity

Readers must navigate the layered structure of nested narratives, keeping track of multiple storylines and narrators.

2. Depth and Perspective

The embedded narratives provide depth and perspective, shedding light on characters' motivations, histories, and hidden truths.

3. Revealing Connections

The interplay between the primary and embedded

narratives often reveals connections and thematic resonances that enrich the overall reading experience.

4. Exploring Interpretation

Readers may find themselves interpreting the narratives, drawing connections, and speculating on the reliability of various narrators.

Stories as Matryoshka Dolls

Nested narratives are like literary matryoshka dolls, each story waiting to be discovered within another. They invite readers to explore the layers of storytelling, uncover hidden depths, and contemplate the intricate relationship between narratives and truth.

As you dive into the world of nested narratives, embrace the sense of discovery and interconnectedness they offer. These stories remind us that there are layers to every tale, and that the act of storytelling is a journey of exploration and revelation. In the end, nested narratives enrich our understanding of the complexities of human experience and the endless possibilities of narrative structure.

Chapter 17
Breaking the Fourth Wall
Engaging the Reader

Picture this: You're engrossed in a book, following the characters' adventures and immersing yourself in the world the author has created. But suddenly, something unexpected happens—the characters turn and address you, the reader, directly. This is the magic of breaking the fourth wall, a literary device that shatters the barrier between fiction and reality. In this chapter, we'll explore the art of breaking the fourth wall, where authors engage readers as active participants in the narrative, creating a unique and immersive reading experience.

What Is Breaking the Fourth Wall?

In the world of theater, the "fourth wall" refers to the imaginary barrier that separates the performers from the audience. When an actor addresses the audience directly, they "break the fourth wall." In literature, breaking the fourth wall occurs when characters, narrators, or the author acknowledge the reader's presence or communicate with them directly.

Engaging the Reader: Techniques and Effects

Breaking the fourth wall is a versatile literary technique that can be used in various ways to achieve different effects:

1. Direct Address

Characters or the narrator speak directly to the reader, often using second-person pronouns like "you." This can create a sense of immediacy and intimacy, as if the characters are confiding in the reader.

2. Commentary

Characters or the narrator may provide commentary on the story, offer explanations, or share insights with the reader. This can serve to enhance the reader's understanding of the narrative.

3. Humor

Breaking the fourth wall can be used for comedic effect, as characters make witty remarks or acknowledge the absurdity of their situation. This can create a playful and lighthearted tone.

4. Self-Reflection

Characters may question their existence as fictional beings or ponder the nature of storytelling. This can lead to philosophical and metafictional discussions within the narrative.

Examples of Breaking the Fourth Wall

Let's explore a few examples of breaking the fourth wall in literature:

1. "To Kill a Mockingbird" by Harper Lee

The novel is narrated by Scout Finch, who reflects on her childhood experiences in the 1930s. At the beginning of the book, an adult Scout addresses the reader, providing insight into her perspective and offering foreshadowing about the events to come.

2. "The Catcher in the Rye" by J.D. Salinger

The protagonist, Holden Caulfield, frequently addresses the reader directly, sharing his thoughts, frustrations, and observations. He even mentions his desire to tell his story to someone — presumably the reader.

3. "House of Leaves" by Mark Z. Danielewski

This novel features multiple layers of narrative, including commentary by a fictional editor who interacts with the reader directly through footnotes and annotations. The format of the book itself breaks the fourth wall, as it includes unconventional typography and formatting.

Challenges and Rewards for Readers

Engaging with literature that breaks the fourth wall offers readers unique challenges and rewards:

1. Immersion

Breaking the fourth wall can make readers feel like active participants in the story, immersing them in the narrative world.

2. Intimacy

The direct address can create a sense of intimacy between the characters and the reader, forging a deeper emotional connection.

3. Reflection

Characters and narrators who engage with the reader can lead to reflections on the nature of storytelling, the role of the reader, and the boundaries between fiction and reality.

4. Playfulness

Breaking the fourth wall can inject humor and playfulness into the narrative, adding an element of surprise and delight.

A Literary Connection

Breaking the fourth wall is a literary device that bridges the gap between the fictional realm and the reader's reality. It invites readers to step inside the narrative, to become more than passive observers but active participants in the storytelling process. As you encounter literature that employs this technique, embrace the unique connection it forges between you and the characters, authors, and the world within the pages.

Ultimately, breaking the fourth wall is a reminder that stories are a form of communication—a dialogue between the author and the reader. It's an invitation to engage, reflect, and explore the boundaries of fiction and reality, creating a literary experience that is both immersive and thought-provoking.

Chapter 18
Stream of Conciousness
Writing the Mind

Imagine stepping inside someone's mind, witnessing the unfiltered flow of thoughts, memories, and sensations as they occur. This is the essence of stream of consciousness, a narrative technique that plunges readers into the inner workings of a character's mind. In this chapter, we'll dive deep into the art of stream of consciousness, exploring how authors use this technique to portray the intricacies of human thought and consciousness, offering a unique and often immersive reading experience.

Defining Stream of Consciousness
The Uninterrupted Flow

Stream of consciousness is a narrative style that aims to replicate the uninterrupted and often chaotic flow of thoughts and sensations experienced by a character. This technique allows readers to observe the character's inner monologue, capturing the immediacy and subjectivity of their mental processes.

Key Characteristics of Stream of Consciousness
1. Unbroken Flow

Stream of consciousness presents thoughts and feelings as they occur, without traditional punctuation or paragraph breaks. This uninterrupted flow mimics the continuous nature of thought.

2. First-Person Perspective

Stream of consciousness is often narrated in the first person, giving readers direct access to the character's inner world. This perspective provides an intimate connection between the reader and the character.

3. Subjectivity

The narrative is highly subjective, reflecting the character's unique perspective, associations, and emotions. It may include fragmented thoughts, memories, and sensory experiences.

4. Free Association

Stream of consciousness often involves free association, where one thought leads to another based on subjective associations rather than a linear or logical progression.

Literary Origins of Stream of Consciousness

While stream of consciousness became prominent in the 20th century, its roots can be traced back to earlier works:

1. James Joyce's "Ulysses" (1922)

Joyce's novel is a landmark in the use of stream of consciousness. The book delves into the minds of its characters, capturing their thoughts, dreams, and memories in a complex narrative that mirrors the structure of Homer's "Odyssey."

2. Virginia Woolf's "Mrs. Dalloway" (1925)

Woolf's novel follows the thoughts and experiences of its protagonist, Clarissa Dalloway, as she prepares for a party. The narrative seamlessly transitions between different characters' inner monologues, providing insight into their perspectives.

Exploring the Mind
Stream of Consciousness in Practice

Stream of consciousness can be employed in various ways to achieve different effects in storytelling:

1. Character Exploration

By immersing readers in a character's inner world, authors can delve deep into their psychology, revealing their fears, desires, and conflicts.

2. Intimacy

The first-person perspective fosters an intimate connection between the reader and the character. Readers become privy to the character's most private thoughts and emotions.

3. Temporal Exploration

Stream of consciousness can explore the fluid nature of time and memory, as characters move seamlessly between past, present, and future experiences.

4. Experimentation

Authors often use stream of consciousness to experiment with narrative structure and language, pushing the boundaries of conventional storytelling.

Examples of Stream of Consciousness

Let's explore a few examples of stream of consciousness in literature:

1. "The Sound and the Fury" by William Faulkner

This novel employs multiple stream-of-consciousness narrators, including Benjy, a character with a cognitive disability. The narrative provides insight into the characters' complex relationships and inner turmoil.

2. "The Catcher in the Rye" by J.D. Salinger

The novel follows the stream of consciousness of its protagonist, Holden Caulfield, as he navigates the challenges of adolescence and alienation. Holden's unfiltered voice captures the raw emotions of youth.

3. "To the Lighthouse" by Virginia Woolf

This novel explores the thoughts and perceptions of its characters, moving between their inner monologues as they grapple with themes of time, loss, and creativity.

Challenges and Rewards for Readers

Engaging with stream of consciousness offers readers a unique set of challenges and rewards:

1. Complexity

The narrative style can be challenging, with fragmented thoughts and nonlinear storytelling. Readers must navigate the character's mind, piecing together the narrative like a puzzle.

2. Intimacy

Readers are granted unparalleled access to a character's innermost thoughts and emotions, forging a deep connection with the protagonist.

3. Exploration

Stream of consciousness allows for the exploration of complex themes, such as identity, memory, and the nature of consciousness itself.

4. Empathy

Readers may gain a deeper understanding of a character's motivations and struggles, fostering empathy and emotional resonance.

The Mind Unveiled

Stream of consciousness is a literary journey into the depths of the human mind, where thoughts flow like a river, unfiltered and unadulterated. It invites readers to explore the innermost recesses of a character's consciousness, offering a profound and often challenging reading experience.

As you encounter works that employ stream of consciousness, embrace the opportunity to step into the minds of characters, to witness their joys and sorrows, and to grapple with the complexities of human thought and emotion. In the end, stream of consciousness reminds us that storytelling can be a mirror held up to the human mind, reflecting its intricacies, mysteries, and endless capacity for introspection.

Chapter 19
Experimental Genre Blending

Imagine walking into a literary buffet where the boundaries between genres blur and blend like flavors in a fusion dish. This is the realm of experimental genre blending, a literary playground where authors challenge the conventions of traditional genre categories, creating narratives that are deliciously complex and delightfully unpredictable. In this chapter, we'll explore the art of experimental genre blending, where authors combine, mix, and remix genres to craft stories that defy easy classification and offer readers a tantalizing taste of the unexpected.

Defining Genre Blending
Beyond the Boundaries

Genre blending is the practice of merging elements of different literary genres within a single narrative. It involves the fusion of themes, styles, and conventions that may traditionally belong to separate genres. This technique allows authors to create narratives that are rich in diversity, complexity, and innovation.

Key Elements of Genre Blending
1. Hybridity

Genre-blending narratives often feature a hybrid approach, combining the characteristics of multiple genres. For example, a story might incorporate elements of science fiction, fantasy, and romance simultaneously.

2. Deconstruction

Authors may deconstruct and subvert genre conventions, challenging reader expectations and reimagining traditional narrative structures.

3. Interplay

Genres can interact and influence each other within the narrative, with elements from one genre affecting the development of another. This interplay adds depth and complexity to the story.

Exploring Experimental Genre Blending

Genre blending can manifest in various ways, depending on the author's creative vision and intent:

1. Mixing Themes

Authors may blend genres by combining themes that are not typically associated with each other. For instance, a crime novel might incorporate elements of spirituality and mysticism.

2. Playing with Tropes

Genre-blending narratives may subvert or remix genre-specific tropes and clichés, creating fresh and unexpected story arcs.

3. Combining Settings

Authors can merge settings from different genres, placing characters in worlds that defy traditional genre boundaries. This can lead to intriguing world-building and unique narrative possibilities.

4. Experimenting with Style

The blending of genres often involves experimenting with narrative style, voice, and tone. The result can be a narrative that shifts seamlessly between different narrative modes.

Examples of Experimental Genre Blending

Let's explore a few examples of experimental genre blending in literature:

1. "The Hitchhiker's Guide to the Galaxy" by Douglas Adams

This iconic science fiction series blends elements of humor, satire, and absurdity with traditional science fiction tropes. The result is a genre-defying narrative that transcends typical sci-fi conventions.

2. "The Night Circus" by Erin Morgenstern

This novel combines elements of fantasy and romance, immersing readers in a magical competition between two young illusionists. The blending of genres creates a dreamlike, enchanting narrative.

3. "Cloud Atlas" by David Mitchell

Mitchell's novel weaves together multiple interconnected stories, each belonging to a different genre, including historical fiction, science fiction, and post-apocalyptic fiction. The result is a narrative tapestry that explores themes of interconnectedness and reincarnation.

Challenges and Rewards for Readers

Engaging with genre-blending narratives offers readers a unique set of challenges and rewards:

1. Surprise and Innovation:

Genre blending often leads to unexpected plot twists and narrative choices, keeping readers engaged and intrigued.

2. Expanded Horizons

Readers are exposed to a wider range of genres and literary traditions, broadening their reading experiences.

3. Thoughtful Reflection

Genre-blending narratives may provoke reflection on the nature of storytelling, the fluidity of genre boundaries, and the power of creative experimentation.

4. Diversity of Themes

Genre blending allows authors to explore a diverse array of themes, often transcending the limitations of a single genre.

Literary Alchemy

Experimental genre blending is a form of literary alchemy, where genres are mixed and transformed into something entirely new and captivating. It invites readers to step out of their comfort zones and explore narratives that are as unpredictable as they are imaginative.

As you embark on your literary journey, seek out genre-blending works that challenge your expectations, broaden your horizons, and remind you of the boundless creativity of authors. In these narratives, you'll discover a world of storytelling possibilities where genres blend, merge, and evolve, offering readers an exhilarating taste of the uncharted and the unexpected.

Chapter 20
Postmodernism and Deconstruction

In the vast landscape of literature, there exists a terrain where the rules of narrative convention are upended, where the very foundations of meaning and reality are questioned. This territory is known as postmodernism, and at its heart lies the philosophical practice of deconstruction. In this chapter, we'll journey into the world of postmodernism and deconstruction, exploring how these movements have reshaped literature by challenging traditional narratives, structures, and interpretations. It's a literary adventure that invites readers to question, reflect, and embrace the complexities of the written word.

Defining Postmodernism: Beyond Modernity

Postmodernism is a complex and multifaceted cultural and literary movement that emerged in the mid-20th century. It is characterized by a rejection of the conventions of modernism and an embrace of ambiguity, pluralism, and self-awareness. Postmodern literature seeks to dismantle traditional notions of authority, hierarchy, and certainty.

Key Characteristics of Postmodernism
1. Metafiction
Postmodern literature often features self-referential elements, blurring the line between fiction and reality. Authors may include themselves as characters or comment on the act of writing within the narrative.

2. Fragmentation
Postmodern narratives frequently employ fragmented structures, nonlinear timelines, and multiple perspectives. This fragmentation mirrors the fragmented nature of contemporary life and human consciousness.

3. Intertextuality
Postmodern texts are intertextual, referencing and drawing upon other texts, genres, and cultural works. This intertextuality invites readers to engage with a web of references and allusions.

4. Irony and Parody
Irony and parody are common in postmodern literature. Authors may use humor and satire to critique cultural, social, and political norms.

The Role of Deconstruction
Unraveling Meaning
Deconstruction is a philosophical and critical approach that underpins much of postmodern thought. Developed by the French philosopher Jacques Derrida, deconstruction is concerned with the examination of language and the destabilization of meaning. It challenges the idea that texts have fixed, inherent meanings.

Key Concepts of Deconstruction
1. Textual Instability
Deconstruction asserts that texts are inherently unstable, with multiple, often contradictory interpretations. Language itself is a shifting and elusive medium.

2. Binary Oppositions
Deconstruction deconstructs binary oppositions (e.g., good vs. evil, presence vs. absence) by revealing the inherent ambiguity and fluidity within these constructs.

3. Différance
Derrida introduced the concept of "différance," a wordplay combining "différer" (to differ) and "déférer" (to defer). It highlights the idea that meaning is constantly deferred and deferred, never arriving at a fixed point.

Examples of Postmodern Literature
Let's explore a few examples of postmodern literature:

1. "Slaughterhouse-Five" by Kurt Vonnegut
This novel employs a fragmented narrative structure, time travel, and metafictional elements to explore the experiences of a soldier, Billy Pilgrim, during World War II. Vonnegut uses these techniques to critique the absurdity of war and the limitations of traditional narrative.

2. "If on a winter's night a traveler" by Italo Calvino
Calvino's novel is a metafictional exploration of the act of reading itself. It consists of multiple nested narratives that challenge the reader's expectations and blur the lines between reality and fiction.

3. "House of Leaves" by Mark Z. Danielewski

This novel features a complex narrative structure with multiple narrators, footnotes, and unconventional typography. It explores themes of identity, reality, and the unknown through a labyrinthine story.

Challenges and Rewards for Readers

Engaging with postmodern literature and deconstruction offers readers a unique set of challenges and rewards:

1. Complexity

Postmodern narratives can be challenging due to their fragmented structures and multiple layers of meaning. Readers must actively participate in the interpretation of the text.

2. Critical Thinking

Postmodern literature encourages critical thinking and reflection on the nature of language, meaning, and representation.

3. Diverse Perspectives

These narratives often incorporate diverse voices and perspectives, inviting readers to consider multiple viewpoints.

4. Intellectual Stimulation

Postmodern literature and deconstruction provide intellectual stimulation and a sense of exploration, as readers navigate the complexities of the text.

Embracing Uncertainty

Postmodernism and deconstruction invite readers

to embrace uncertainty, ambiguity, and the ever-shifting nature of meaning. In a world where absolutes are challenged and hierarchies dismantled, literature becomes a space for inquiry, contemplation, and the celebration of the myriad possibilities of language.

As you explore the world of postmodern literature and deconstruction, approach it with an open mind and a willingness to grapple with ambiguity. These movements remind us that the act of reading is an act of interpretation, and that literature has the power to challenge, provoke, and expand our understanding of the world and ourselves.

Chapter 21
Subverting Expectations
The Shock Factor

Have you ever picked up a book, expecting one thing, only to be jolted into a completely unexpected narrative direction? This electrifying literary phenomenon is often the result of authors skillfully subverting expectations, using surprise and shock to propel their stories into uncharted territories. In this chapter, we'll explore the art of subverting expectations, where authors challenge conventional storytelling norms, keeping readers on the edge of their seats and defying predictability.

Defying Predictability: The Power of Subversion

Subverting expectations is a storytelling technique where authors intentionally deviate from established narrative conventions and reader expectations. It's a way to surprise, challenge, and engage readers by taking them into unfamiliar narrative terrain.

Key Elements of Subverting Expectations
1. Plot Twists

Authors introduce unexpected plot twists that defy typical story arcs. These twists can upend character motivations, reveal hidden secrets, or completely change the direction of the narrative.

2. Character Development

Characters may undergo unexpected transformations or reveal hidden depths that challenge reader assumptions.

3. Genre Subversion

Authors play with genre conventions, blending or subverting them to create fresh and surprising narratives.

4. Moral Ambiguity

Subversion can introduce moral ambiguity, forcing readers to reevaluate their allegiances and beliefs.

Narrative Techniques for Subversion

Authors employ various narrative techniques to subvert expectations effectively:

1. Misdirection

Authors lead readers down one narrative path while secretly preparing a surprising twist in another direction.

2. Unreliable Narration

Narrators may be intentionally unreliable, causing readers to question the accuracy of their accounts.

3. Foil Characters

Characters with contrasting qualities may subvert reader expectations by defying stereotypes and playing unexpected roles in the story.

Examples of Subverting Expectations

Let's explore a few examples of subverting expectations in literature:

1. "Gone Girl" by Gillian Flynn

This psychological thriller subverts expectations by presenting alternating viewpoints of a married couple, Nick and Amy. As the narrative unfolds, it challenges readers' perceptions of truth, marriage, and character motivations through shocking revelations.

2. "Fight Club" by Chuck Palahniuk

Palahniuk's novel subverts expectations through its unreliable narrator and an identity-twisting plot. The story ultimately challenges readers to question the boundaries of self and society.

3. "The Road" by Cormac McCarthy

While the post-apocalyptic setting of "The Road" leads readers to expect a bleak narrative, McCarthy subverts expectations by emphasizing the father-son relationship and moments of tenderness amid the harsh landscape.

Challenges and Rewards for Readers

Engaging with narratives that subvert expectations offers readers a unique set of challenges and rewards:

1. Intellectual Engagement

Subverted narratives demand active reader engagement, encouraging them to analyze, question, and interpret the text more deeply.

2. Emotional Impact

Unexpected twists and character developments can evoke strong emotional responses, from shock and anger to empathy and understanding.

3. Critical Thinking

Subverted narratives often provoke critical thinking, challenging readers to reassess their assumptions about characters, plot, and themes.

4. Expanded Horizons

Exposure to unexpected narrative choices broadens readers' horizons and encourages them to explore new literary territory.

The Art of Surprise

Subverting expectations is the art of literary surprise, where authors act as magicians, pulling narrative rabbits out of hats. It's a reminder that storytelling is not bound by rigid conventions but is a dynamic, ever-evolving art form. As you encounter narratives that subvert expectations, relish the shock, embrace the unpredictability, and savor the journey into uncharted narrative territory.

These stories invite you to expect the unexpected, reminding you that literature's power lies not only in the familiar but also in the startling, the unconventional, and the transformative. So, keep turning the pages, for the next twist may just be the one that leaves you breathless and forever changed by the world of words.

Chapter 22
Crafting Your Experimental Story

Throughout this book, we've embarked on a literary journey exploring experimental storytelling and the myriad ways authors push the boundaries of conventional narratives. Now, it's time to put pen to paper—or fingers to keyboard—and embark on your own creative voyage.

In this chapter, we'll guide you through the process of crafting your experimental story, providing insights, tips, and inspiration to help you break free from traditional molds and explore the vast landscape of literary innovation.

1. Define Your Vision

Before you dive into writing, take a moment to clarify your vision for your experimental story. What themes, emotions, or ideas do you want to explore? Are there specific genres or literary techniques you'd like to blend or subvert? Having a clear sense of purpose and direction will guide your creative process.

2. Explore Narrative Techniques

Experimental storytelling offers a wide array of narrative techniques to choose from. Consider which ones align with your vision for the story. Some options to explore include:

Nonlinear Narratives

Play with time and chronology, weaving past, present, and future into a nontraditional structure.

Fragmented Narratives

Create a mosaic of narrative fragments that readers must piece together.

Multiple Perspectives

Tell your story from different characters' viewpoints to offer varied insights and interpretations.

Unreliable Narrators

Craft a narrator whose perspective is skewed or questionable, inviting readers to question the narrative's reliability.

Metafiction

Break the fourth wall, blurring the lines between fiction and reality.

Genre Blending

Combine elements from different genres to create a unique narrative flavor.

3. Develop Complex Characters

Your characters are the heart of your story. Develop well-rounded, multifaceted characters with their own desires, conflicts, and arcs. Subvert character stereotypes and expectations to add depth and intrigue to your narrative.

4. Embrace Themes and Symbolism

Consider the themes and symbolism you want

to incorporate into your story. These can add layers of meaning and complexity to your narrative. Explore how your experimental techniques can enhance or subvert these themes.

5. Experiment with Language

Language is a powerful tool in experimental storytelling. Play with language, style, and voice to create a narrative that is uniquely yours. Don't be afraid to experiment with unconventional grammar, punctuation, and typography if it serves your narrative goals.

6. Balance Innovation and Cohesion

While experimentation is key, strive for a balance between innovation and cohesion. Your story should still be engaging and comprehensible to readers. Ensure that your narrative choices serve the overall story and don't become distractions.

7. Revise and Refine

Experimental storytelling often benefits from careful revision. After completing your initial draft, take the time to review and refine your work. Pay attention to pacing, clarity, and the impact of your experimental techniques on the reader's experience.

8. Seek Feedback

Share your experimental story with trusted readers or writing groups. Their feedback can offer valuable insights and help you refine your narrative choices.

9. Embrace Risk and Uncertainty

Experimental storytelling involves taking risks and embracing uncertainty. Not every reader may connect with your narrative, and that's okay. The beauty of experimentation is that it challenges conventions and invites diverse interpretations.

10. Keep Exploring

Even as you craft your own experimental story, continue exploring the works of other authors who have ventured into the realm of innovation and experimentation. Inspiration often arises from exposure to different styles and ideas.

Your Literary Adventure

Crafting your experimental story is a literary adventure that invites you to explore uncharted territories of creativity and expression. Embrace the freedom to challenge norms, subvert expectations, and push the boundaries of storytelling. Your unique voice and perspective can contribute to the rich tapestry of experimental literature.

Remember that experimentation is not about conforming to rules but about breaking free from them. So, take risks, unleash your imagination, and embark on your own narrative journey. Whether you choose to subvert, blend, deconstruct, or invent, the world of experimental storytelling is yours to explore, and your story is waiting to be told.

Chapter 23
Overcoming Challenges

Every journey, including the creative one, comes with its share of challenges. As you embark on the path of experimental storytelling, you may encounter hurdles, doubts, and moments of frustration. But fear not, for in this chapter, we'll explore common challenges faced by writers of experimental fiction and provide you with strategies and insights to help you overcome them. Let's dive into the heart of the creative struggle and emerge stronger on the other side.

1. Navigating Complexity
Challenge: Experimental storytelling often involves intricate narrative structures, multiple perspectives, and unconventional techniques. Balancing complexity while keeping the story accessible can be challenging.

Solution: Start with a clear vision of your story's core message and themes. Ensure that every experimental choice serves these central elements. Seek feedback from beta readers to gauge whether your narrative complexity enhances or detracts from the reader's experience.

2. Reader Engagement
Challenge: Experimentation can sometimes distance readers if they feel lost or disconnected from the narrative. Keeping readers engaged is crucial.

Solution: Maintain a strong emotional core in your story. Ensure that characters are relatable and their struggles resonate with readers. Balance experimental elements with moments of clarity and connection to sustain reader interest.

3. Balancing Innovation and Cohesion
Challenge: Striking the right balance between innovation and a cohesive narrative can be tricky. Too much experimentation may alienate readers, while too little may make your story feel conventional.

Solution: Consistently refer back to your story's central themes and message. Evaluate whether each experimental choice serves these core elements. Experimentation should enhance, not distract from, your storytelling goals.

4. Risk of Misinterpretation
Challenge: Experimentation can lead to multiple interpretations, and readers may not always grasp your intended message. The risk of misinterpretation can be frustrating.

Solution: Embrace ambiguity as part of the experimental storytelling process. Use symbolism, themes, and motifs to guide readers toward your intended meaning without spelling it out explicitly. Encourage readers to engage with your narrative on their own terms.

5. Rejection and Criticism
Challenge: Not all readers, editors, or publishers may appreciate or understand experimental fiction. Rejection and criticism are par for the course.

Solution: Develop a resilient mindset. Remember that experimental storytelling is not universally loved, and that's okay. Seek out communities of writers and readers who appreciate and understand your style. Keep submitting your work, as the right audience and recognition may be just around the corner.

6. Self-Doubt

Challenge: As an experimental writer, you may question your own choices and wonder if your work is too unconventional or niche.

Solution: Trust your creative instincts. Remember that the literary world has room for a diverse range of voices and styles. Find validation in the joy of experimentation and the satisfaction of pushing boundaries.

7. Finding Your Voice

Challenge: It can take time to discover your unique voice in experimental storytelling. You may feel like you're imitating other authors or struggling to find your authentic style.

Solution: Don't rush the process. Experiment with different techniques and styles. Read widely within the experimental genre to gain insights and inspiration. Over time, your distinctive voice will emerge.

8. Creative Blocks

Challenge: Just like writers of traditional fiction, you may encounter creative blocks or moments when inspiration seems elusive.

Solution: Experimentation thrives on curiosity and

exploration. When you're stuck, try stepping away from your work and immersing yourself in other creative pursuits, such as art, music, or nature. Inspiration often strikes when you least expect it.

9. Fear of Failure
Challenge: The fear of "getting it wrong" or producing a story that falls flat can be paralyzing.

Solution: Embrace the idea that experimentation inherently involves risk. Failure is a natural part of the creative process and can lead to growth and discovery. The most groundbreaking works often arise from taking bold risks.

10. Persistence
Challenge: Writing experimental fiction can be a long and challenging journey, and it's easy to become discouraged.

Solution: Stay persistent and patient. Remember why you were drawn to experimental storytelling in the first place. Celebrate your small victories, and view challenges as opportunities for growth and learning.

The Creative Odyssey

Writing experimental fiction is not for the faint of heart, but it is a rewarding and transformative creative journey. Embrace the challenges as opportunities to evolve as a writer and thinker. Keep experimenting, pushing boundaries, and exploring the vast possibilities of storytelling. In the end, it's the resilience and passion of the experimental writer that lead to literary breakthroughs and unforgettable narratives.

Chapter 24
Showcasing Your Unique Voice

In the realm of experimental storytelling, your unique voice is your most powerful tool. It's the fingerprint that sets your narrative apart, the signature that distinguishes your work from others. In this chapter, we'll explore how to embrace and showcase your unique voice in your experimental writing. Your voice is a precious asset, and when nurtured and celebrated, it can transform your stories into unforgettable literary experiences.

1. Embrace Your Authenticity

Your unique voice begins with embracing your authenticity as a writer. Don't try to mimic the styles or techniques of other authors. Instead, recognize that your perspective, experiences, and insights are valuable and worth sharing. Authenticity is the cornerstone of a powerful voice.

2. Explore Your Interests and Passions

Consider what truly excites and engages you as a writer. What topics, themes, or ideas are you passionate about? Your unique voice often emerges when you explore subjects that genuinely resonate with you. Whether it's a fascination with science, a love of history, or a passion for the human condition, let your interests guide your writing.

3. Experiment Boldly

As an experimental writer, you have the freedom to push the boundaries of storytelling. Don't be afraid to experiment boldly with narrative techniques, styles, and structures. Your voice can shine through when you take risks and explore uncharted territory.

4. Develop a Distinctive Style

Your writing style is a crucial component of your voice. Whether you favor concise and poetic prose, long and flowing sentences, or a minimalist approach, your style should reflect your personality and your narrative's needs. Experiment with different styles to find the one that resonates with you.

5. Create Memorable Characters

The characters you create are a reflection of your voice. Develop characters that are distinct, relatable, and layered. Explore their motivations, quirks, and complexities. Your characters can carry your voice through the narrative, making it unforgettable.

6. Craft Unique Dialogues

Dialogue is a powerful tool for showcasing your voice. Develop dialogues that are authentic to your characters and the world you've created. Experiment with speech patterns, rhythms, and idiosyncrasies to make your characters' voices distinctive.

7. Use Symbolism and Imagery

Symbolism and imagery are vehicles for expressing your voice on a deeper level. Incorporate symbols and vivid descriptions that resonate with your themes and message. These elements can infuse your narrative with layers of meaning.

8. Invite Readers into Your Mind

In experimental storytelling, it's often beneficial to invite readers into your mind and thought processes. Use techniques like stream of consciousness, inner monologue, or first-person narration to immerse readers in your characters' inner worlds and thought processes. This intimacy can create a strong connection between your voice and your readers.

9. Seek Feedback and Refinement

Share your work with trusted readers, writing groups, or mentors. Their feedback can provide valuable insights into how your voice is coming across and how it can be further refined. Be open to constructive criticism while staying true to your artistic vision.

10. Evolve and Grow

A unique voice is not static; it evolves and grows over time. Continue to read widely, experiment with new techniques, and challenge yourself as a writer. Your voice will naturally evolve as you gain experience and explore different aspects of storytelling.

Your Voice, Your Legacy

Your unique voice is your literary legacy. It's the imprint you leave on the world of storytelling, the echo of your thoughts and emotions in the minds of your readers. It's a gift to be nurtured, celebrated, and shared with the world.

As you continue your journey as an experimental writer, remember that your voice is a beacon of creativity, a vessel for authenticity, and a bridge between your imagination and your readers' hearts. It's your voice that makes your stories resonate, your narratives unforgettable, and your mark on the world of literature enduring. So, write fearlessly, experiment relentlessly, and let your unique voice shine brightly in the tapestry of storytelling.

Chapter 25
The Future of Experimental Storytelling

As we stand on the threshold of the future, the world of storytelling continues to evolve and expand. Experimental storytelling, with its penchant for innovation and pushing boundaries, is no exception. In this chapter, we'll peer into the crystal ball and explore the exciting possibilities and emerging trends that may shape the future of experimental storytelling. From the fusion of technology and narrative to the democratization of storytelling, the journey ahead promises to be as exhilarating as it is unpredictable.

1. The Fusion of Technology and Narrative

The marriage of technology and storytelling is set to redefine the landscape of experimental narrative. Augmented reality (AR), virtual reality (VR), interactive narratives, and immersive experiences are becoming increasingly accessible to creators. These technologies offer new dimensions for experimentation, allowing readers to step into the story world, interact with characters, and explore narratives in unprecedented ways.

2. Interactive and Participatory Storytelling

The future holds exciting prospects for interactive storytelling, where readers actively shape the narrative.

Interactive fiction, choose-your-own-adventure stories, and branching narratives are gaining popularity. Emerging platforms and tools make it easier for authors to craft dynamic, user-driven experiences.

3. Transmedia Storytelling

Transmedia storytelling, where a narrative unfolds across multiple media platforms (e.g., books, films, games, social media), is poised for growth. Creators are using this approach to immerse audiences in rich, multifaceted story worlds that extend far beyond the confines of a single medium.

4. Inclusivity and Diverse Voices

The future of experimental storytelling is inherently diverse and inclusive. As barriers to entry continue to crumble, writers from marginalized communities are finding their voices and contributing unique perspectives to the narrative landscape. Their stories challenge traditional narratives and enrich the world of experimental storytelling.

5. Environmental and Interactive Storytelling

With increasing awareness of environmental issues, storytelling is becoming a powerful tool for advocacy and change. Interactive narratives that encourage readers to explore ecological themes and engage in environmental issues are on the rise. These narratives serve not only as a form of entertainment but also as a means to educate and inspire action.

6. The Hybridization of Genres

Genre boundaries continue to blur as experimental storytellers explore the fusion of disparate genres. Expect to see more genre-defying narratives that combine elements of science fiction, fantasy, horror, and more. This trend challenges conventional categorizations and delights readers with fresh and unexpected storytelling.

7. The Power of Collaboration

The future may see increased collaboration among writers, visual artists, musicians, and creators from various disciplines. These collaborations can result in multimedia storytelling experiences that transcend traditional boundaries and engage multiple senses.

8. The Rise of Microfiction and Flash Fiction

In our fast-paced world, shorter forms of storytelling are gaining popularity. Microfiction and flash fiction challenge writers to distill powerful narratives into concise, impactful pieces. These bite-sized stories are ideal for the digital age and can be easily shared on social media platforms.

9. Reimagining Classic Works

Expect to see more reinterpretations and reimaginings of classic literary works through an experimental lens. Writers will continue to explore how these timeless tales can be reshaped and reinvigorated to reflect contemporary sensibilities and themes.

10. The Democratization of Storytelling

The democratization of storytelling, thanks to the internet and digital tools, is a driving force in the future of experimental narrative. Aspiring writers and creators have unprecedented access to global audiences, allowing for a diversity of voices and stories to flourish.

A World of Boundless Possibility

The future of experimental storytelling is a tapestry woven with threads of innovation, diversity, and limitless potential. As we look ahead, we anticipate narratives that engage our senses, challenge our perceptions, and invite us to actively participate in the storytelling process.

As a writer and reader, you are a vital part of this future. Embrace the spirit of experimentation, be open to new technologies, and celebrate the diversity of voices that will shape the narrative landscape. Your imagination is the compass that will guide you through this exciting frontier of storytelling, where the only limit is the boundless horizon of your creativity. The future of experimental storytelling awaits your unique voice and vision.

Chapter 26
Embracing Innovation in Your Writing

Innovation is the lifeblood of experimental storytelling. It's the driving force that propels the narrative into uncharted territory, challenging conventions and reshaping the boundaries of literature. As we conclude our journey through this book, we'll delve into the heart of innovation and explore how you can infuse your writing with creativity, freshness, and a sense of exploration.

Whether you're an experienced writer or just starting your literary voyage, the principles of innovation can breathe new life into your storytelling.

1. Cultivate Curiosity

The first step in embracing innovation is to cultivate curiosity. Be inquisitive about the world around you. Question assumptions and conventions. Explore a wide range of interests, from science and art to history and philosophy. The more you feed your curiosity, the richer your well of inspiration becomes.

2. Experiment with Style

Innovation often begins with experimenting with your writing style. Don't be afraid to venture outside your comfort zone. Try different narrative voices, perspectives, and tenses. Mix the formal with the informal, the lyrical with the stark. Each experiment is an opportunity for growth and discovery.

3. Play with Structure

Structure is a powerful tool for innovation. Experiment with different narrative structures, timelines, and formats. Consider nonlinear narratives, fragmented storytelling, or even mixing media like letters, diaries, and multimedia elements. The structure can be as much a part of the story as the plot itself.

4. Harness the Power of Language

Language is your palette, and words are your brushes. Experiment with language to create vivid, evocative imagery and thought-provoking prose. Play with metaphors, similes, and symbolism. Develop your own writing rituals and exercises to keep your language fresh and inventive.

5. Explore Themes and Motifs

Innovation extends to the themes and motifs you explore in your writing. Don't shy away from challenging or unconventional topics. Dive into the human experience, from the mundane to the extraordinary. Themes that resonate on a universal level often yield the most innovative narratives.

6. Cross Genres and Boundaries

Innovation thrives at the intersections of genres and boundaries. Consider blending genres or fusing elements from different literary traditions. These hybrid narratives can breathe new life into familiar storytelling conventions.

7. Embrace Collaboration

Collaboration can be a wellspring of innovation. Partner with artists, musicians, or creators from other disciplines. Their perspectives and skills can inspire fresh approaches to your writing. Together, you can craft multimedia narratives that push the boundaries of traditional storytelling.

8. Seek Inspiration Everywhere

Inspiration can strike from the most unexpected places. Keep your senses open to the world around you. Travel, explore nature, visit museums, and engage in conversations with people from diverse backgrounds. The experiences you gather can infuse your writing with unique perspectives and fresh ideas.

9. Challenge Yourself

Pushing the boundaries of your comfort zone is a hallmark of innovation. Challenge yourself with writing prompts, constraints, or word limits. Join writing communities or workshops that encourage experimentation. The act of challenging yourself fosters creativity and growth.

10. Embrace Failure as Growth

Not every experiment will yield a masterpiece, and that's perfectly fine. Embrace failure as an essential part of the creative process. Learn from your missteps, refine your approach, and use your failures as stepping stones toward innovation.

Your Creative Odyssey Continues

Embracing innovation in your writing is an ongoing, dynamic journey. It's a process of constant discovery, evolution, and transformation. As you apply these principles of innovation, remember that your unique voice and perspective are your greatest assets.

The world of experimental storytelling is a vast and ever-expanding landscape, and you are an intrepid explorer charting its uncharted territories. Keep pushing boundaries, challenging conventions, and infusing your writing with the spark of innovation. Your creative odyssey is an infinite adventure, and the stories you craft have the power to inspire, provoke, and captivate. The future of literature is yours to shape, one innovative word at a time.

Writing Prompts

Innovation often begins with a spark of inspiration. Use these writing prompts to ignite your creativity and explore new narrative possibilities:

1. Write a story that unfolds entirely in reverse chronological order, starting with the end and concluding with the beginning.

2. Create a character who perceives the world through synesthesia, blending sensory experiences in unique ways.

3. Craft a story where the narrator is an inanimate object, such as a photograph, a mirror, or a diary.

4. Write a narrative that incorporates elements of found documents, such as newspaper clippings, letters, or social media posts.

5. Experiment with a story told entirely through dialogue, with no narrative descriptions or attributions.

6. Develop a story where the protagonist is an unreliable narrator, and the reader must decipher the truth from their skewed perspective.

7. Create a narrative that takes place entirely within the confines of a single room. Explore how the setting influences the story.

8. Write a story in the second person, addressing the reader directly and immersing them in the narrative.

9. Craft a microfiction piece (under 100 words) that conveys a complete story or evokes powerful emotions.

10. Experiment with a story that incorporates elements of magical realism, blurring the boundaries between the mundane and the fantastical.

Recommended Reading List

Expand your horizons and dive deeper into the world of experimental storytelling with these recommended books and authors:

1. **"House of Leaves" by Mark Z. Danielewski:** A labyrinthine narrative that explores the layers of reality through unconventional formatting and storytelling techniques.

2. **"If on a winter's night a traveler" by Italo Calvino:** A metafictional masterpiece that invites readers on a journey through various narrative fragments and genres.

3. **"The Raw Shark Texts" by Steven Hall:** A mind-bending narrative featuring a protagonist who battles a conceptual shark in the sea of language.

4. **"Infinite Jest" by David Foster Wallace:** A dense, complex novel known for its intricate narrative structure and exploration of addiction, entertainment, and tennis.

5. **"The Famished Road" by Ben Okri:** A blend of magical realism and social commentary set in Nigeria, featuring a spirit-child protagonist.

6. **"The Wind-Up Bird Chronicle" by Haruki Murakami:**

A surreal exploration of identity, loss, and reality that weaves multiple narrative threads.

7. "S." by J.J. Abrams and Doug Dorst: A novel within a novel, filled with annotations, letters, and ephemera, creating an interactive reading experience.

8. "Hopscotch" by Julio Cortázar: A narrative that invites readers to choose their own path through the story, experiencing it in multiple ways.

9. "The Night Circus" by Erin Morgenstern: A lush, atmospheric tale that combines elements of fantasy and romance in a unique and enchanting narrative.

10. "Pale Fire" by Vladimir Nabokov: A complex work featuring a poem, commentary, and unreliable narrator, blurring the lines between fiction and reality.

Publishing Your Experimental Work

Getting your experimental work published is an exciting step in your writing journey. Here are some practical tips for navigating the publishing process:

1. Research Literary Journals: Look for literary journals and magazines that specialize in experimental or unconventional fiction. Submissions to these publications are often open to experimental works.

2. Prepare a Strong Submission: When submitting your work, carefully follow the submission guidelines provided by the publication. Craft a compelling cover letter and format your manuscript professionally.

3. Consider Small Presses: Independent and small presses may be more open to experimental works than larger publishing houses. Explore opportunities with these publishers.

4. Self-Publishing: If you prefer full creative control, consider self-publishing your work as an e-book or print-on-demand book. Platforms like Amazon Kindle Direct Publishing and IngramSpark offer accessible options.

5. Connect with the Writing Community: Attend writing conferences, workshops, and literary events to network with fellow writers and publishers. Building connections in the writing community can open doors to publishing opportunities.

6. Writer's Residencies and Grants: Look for writer's residencies and grants that support experimental writers. These programs can provide valuable time and resources for your creative projects.

7. Keep Submitting: Rejections are a natural part of the publishing process. Don't be discouraged by rejection letters; keep submitting your work to different publications and opportunities.

Writing Exercises and Workshops

Enhance your skills and expand your horizons through writing exercises and workshops. These resources offer valuable opportunities for growth and experimentation:

1. Online Writing Communities: Join online writing communities where writers share prompts, feedback, and discussions on experimental writing techniques.

2. Local Writing Groups: Seek out local writing groups or workshops that focus on experimental storytelling. Engaging with peers can provide valuable support and feedback.

3. Creative Writing Courses: Enroll in creative writing courses at universities or online platforms. Many courses cover experimental writing techniques.

4. Writing Retreats: Consider attending a writing retreat or residency program focused on experimentation and innovation. These immersive experiences can be transformative for your writing.

5. Writing Exercises: Explore books and resources on that encourage experimentation. Try exercises that challenge you to break free from traditional narrative structures.

Glossary of Experimental Storytelling Terms

Expand your vocabulary and understanding of experimental storytelling with this glossary of key terms and concepts:

1. Metafiction: Fiction that self-consciously addresses its own nature as a narrative, often breaking the fourth wall and blurring the lines between fiction and reality.

2. Oulipo: A literary movement that uses constrained writing techniques to spark creativity, such as using specific mathematical or linguistic constraints.

3. Ergodic Literature: Texts that require non-trivial effort from the reader to understand the narrative, often involving unconventional formatting or navigation.

4. Narrative Frame: A story within a story, where one narrative contains or surrounds another, creating layers of storytelling.

5. Asemic Writing: Writing that lacks specific semantic content, relying on abstract symbols or visual aesthetics to convey meaning.

6. Found Poetry: Poetry created by selecting and rearranging words or phrases from existing texts, such as newspapers or dictionaries.

7. Cut-Up Technique: A method of experimental writing where existing texts are cut into pieces and rearranged to create new, often surreal narratives.

8. Concrete Poetry: Poetry that uses visual arrangement of words and letters to enhance the meaning and impact of the poem.

9. Collage Narratives: Narratives that incorporate elements from various sources, such as images, texts, and objects, to create a cohesive story.

10. Hypertext Fiction: Digital narratives that use hyperlinks to allow readers to choose their own path through the story, creating a nonlinear reading experience.

Resources for Further Exploration

Continue your exploration of experimental storytelling with these additional resources:

1. Websites and Blogs: Explore websites and blogs dedicated to experimental literature and writing, such as "Electronic Literature Organization" (eliterature.org) and "UbuWeb" (ubu.com).

2. Literary Magazines: Subscribe to literary magazines that feature experimental works, such as "Conjunctions," "Black Warrior Review," and "NOÖ Journal."

3. Writing Software: Utilize writing software and tools that facilitate experimentation, such as Scrivener, Twine, and Inklewriter for interactive fiction.

4. Library Resources: Visit your local library to discover books, journals, and academic publications on experimental literature and writing techniques.

5. Conferences and Festivals: Attend literary conferences and festivals focused on experimental storytelling, such as the "Electronic Literature Organization Conference" and "ELO's Media Arts Show."

www.ingramcontent.com/pod-product-compliance
Lightning Source LLC
Chambersburg PA
CBHW070029300526
45794CB00001B/437